How to Use This Book

Look for these special features in this book:

SIDEBARS, **CHARTS**, **GRAPHS**, and original **MAPS** expand your understanding of what's being discussed—and also make useful sources for classroom reports.

FAQs answer common **F**requently **A**sked **Q**uestions about people, places, and things.

WOW FACTORS offer "Who knew?" facts to keep you thinking.

TRAVEL GUIDE gives you tips on exploring the state—either in person or right from your chair!

PROJECT ROOM provides fun ideas for school assignments and incredible research projects. Plus, there's a guide to primary sources—what they are and how to cite them.

Please note: All statistics are as up-to-date as possible at the time of publication. Population data is taken from the 2010 census.

Consultants: Mella Harmon, Curator of History, Nevada Historical Society, and Managing Editor, *Nevada Historical Society Quarterly;* William Loren Katz; Daphne D. LaPointe, Research Geologist, Economic Geology, Nevada Bureau of Mines and Geology, University of Nevada– Reno; Crystal Van Dee, Curator of Manuscripts, Nevada State Museum

Book production by The Design Lab

Library of Congress Cataloging-in-Publication Data
Heinrichs, Ann.
 Nevada / Ann Heinrichs. — Revised edition.
  pages cm. — (America, the beautiful. Third series)
 Includes bibliographical references and index.
 ISBN 978-0-531-24893-5 (lib. bdg.)
 1. Nevada—Juvenile literature. I. Title.
 F841.3.H45 2014
 979.3—dc23   2013032828

2 3 4 5 6 7 8 9 10 R 23 22 21 20 19 18 17 16 15

Revised Edition

AMERICA ★ THE ★ BEAUTIFUL

Nevada

BY ANN HEINRICHS

Third Series, Revised Edition

Children's Press®
A Division of Scholastic Inc.
New York ★ Toronto ★ London ★ Auckland ★ Sydney
Mexico City ★ New Delhi ★ Hong Kong
Danbury, Connecticut

CONTENTS

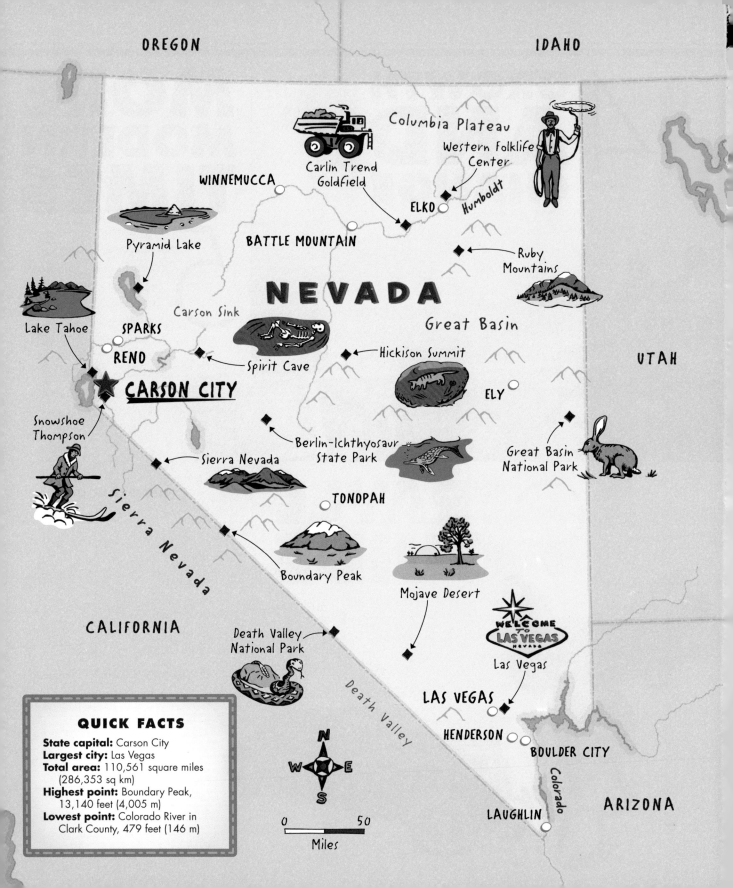

OREGON

IDAHO

Columbia Plateau

Carlin Trend
Goldfield

Western Folklife
Center

WINNEMUCCA

ELKO   Humboldt

Ruby
Mountains

Pyramid Lake

BATTLE MOUNTAIN

NEVADA

Carson Sink

Great Basin

Lake Tahoe

SPARKS

RENO

Spirit Cave

Hickison Summit

ELY

UTAH

CARSON CITY

Snowshoe
Thompson

Sierra Nevada

Berlin-Ichthyosaur
State Park

Great Basin
National Park

Sierra Nevada

TONOPAH

Boundary Peak

Mojave Desert

CALIFORNIA

Death Valley
National Park

WELCOME TO LAS VEGAS NEVADA

Las Vegas

Death Valley

LAS VEGAS

HENDERSON

BOULDER CITY

Colorado

LAUGHLIN

ARIZONA

QUICK FACTS

State capital: Carson City
Largest city: Las Vegas
Total area: 110,561 square miles
(286,353 sq km)
Highest point: Boundary Peak,
13,140 feet (4,005 m)
Lowest point: Colorado River in
Clark County, 479 feet (146 m)

N
W   E
S

0   50
Miles

Welcome to Nevada!

HOW DID NEVADA GET ITS NAME?

What does *Nevada* mean? It's Spanish for "snowy" or "snow-covered." That may seem like an odd name for a desertlike state. But you have to hear the whole story.

In 1776, Spaniard Padre Pedro Font was traveling in northern California. Far in the distance to the east, he spied the snowy peaks of a mountain range. He named them the Sierra Nevada. That's Spanish for "snow-covered mountains." Those mountains rise on Nevada's western border with California.

What is now called Nevada was once known as Washoe, after the Washoe group of Native Americans who lived there. In 1861, the area became a U.S. territory. Some residents wanted the new territory to be named Washoe Territory. Others wanted it to be named after the glistening peaks of the Sierra Nevada. The name *Nevada* won!

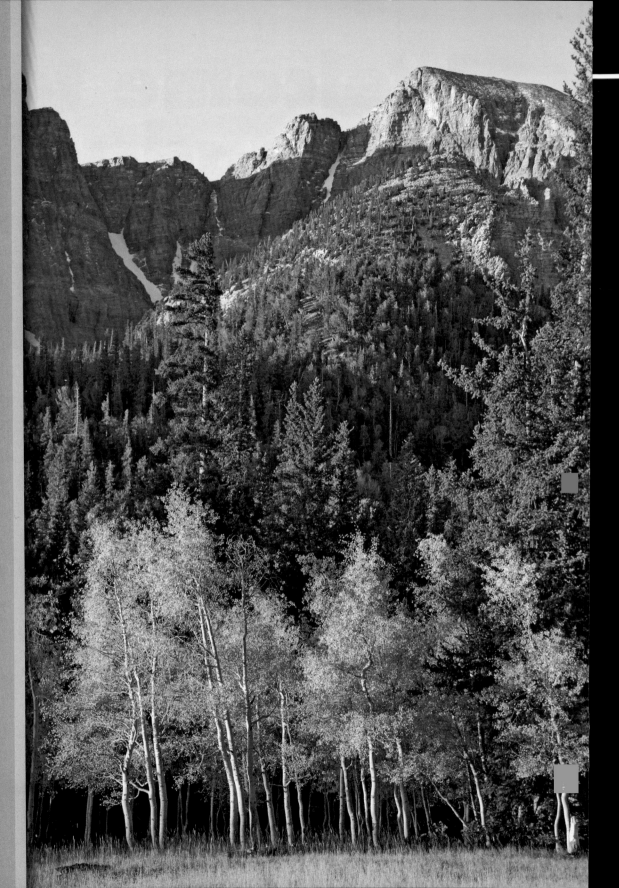

READ ABOUT

Fall colors at
Wheeler Peak
in Nevada's
Great Basin
National Park

CHAPTER ONE

LAND

★

PICTURE VAST STRETCHES OF STARK DESERT DOTTED WITH SAGEBRUSH. Add in craggy canyons, snowcapped mountains, occasional grasslands and lush valleys, and sparkling lakes and streams. This is Nevada! Like most western states, Nevada is large. In fact, at 110,561 square miles (286,353 square kilometers) it's the seventh-largest state in the country. Nevada's lowest point, 479 feet (146 meters), is in its southern tip. Near the border of its cut-off left corner, Nevada's highest point, Boundary Peak, reaches to 13,140 feet (4,005 m).

LAND REGIONS

California borders Nevada to the west and southwest. To the east is Utah, and Arizona is to the southeast. Oregon and Idaho lie along Nevada's northern border.

To get an idea of Nevada's geography, imagine a big, shallow bowl. This bowl occupies a rugged stretch of land between the Wasatch Mountains in Utah, to the east, and the Sierra Nevada, to the west. The land between those two mountain ranges is called the Great Basin. It's a large, arid area in the western United States.

Although almost all of Nevada lies within the Great Basin, there are a few minor exceptions in the landscape around the edges of the state. Nevada's southern tip lies in the Mojave Desert; a sliver of the state's northeastern corner is in the Columbia Plateau; and Nevada's western border includes a small piece of the Sierra Nevada.

Nevada Geo-Facts

Along with the state's geographical highlights, this chart ranks Nevada's land, water, and total area compared to all other states.

Total area; rank	110,561 square miles (286,353 sq km); 7th
Land; rank	109,826 square miles (284,449 sq km); 7th
Water; rank	735 square miles (1,904 sq km); 35th
Inland water; rank	735 square miles (1,904 sq km); 29th
Geographic center	Lander County, 26 miles (42 km) southeast of Austin
Latitude	35° N and 42° N
Longitude	114° W and 120° W
Highest point	Boundary Peak, 13,140 feet (4,005 m)
Lowest point	Colorado River in Clark County, 479 feet (146 m)
Largest city	Las Vegas
Number of counties	17
Longest river	Humboldt River, 500 miles (805 km)

Source: U.S. Census Bureau, 2010 census

Only six other states are larger than Nevada. Rhode Island could fit inside Nevada more than 70 times!

The Great Basin

This is sometimes called Nevada's Basin and Range region. Much of Utah and parts of Oregon, California, Wyoming, and Idaho are in the Great Basin, too. Actually, the Great Basin is not just one big bowl. It's a group of many enclosed basins whose waters generally flow inward.

Most Nevada rivers have no outlet toward the sea. Some rivers empty into permanent lakes,

Nevada Topography

Use the color-coded elevation chart to see Nevada's high points (dark red to orange) and low points (green to dark green). Elevation is measured as the distance above or below sea level.

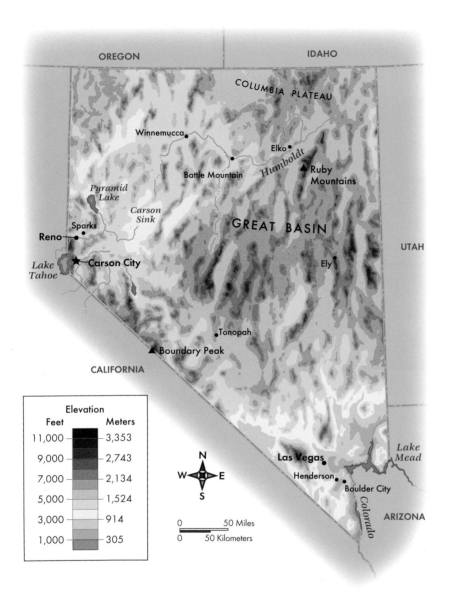

OREGON

IDAHO

COLUMBIA PLATEAU

Winnemucca

Elko

Battle Mountain

Humboldt

Ruby Mountains

Pyramid Lake

Carson Sink

GREAT BASIN

UTAH

Sparks

Reno

Lake Tahoe

Carson City

Ely

Tonopah

Boundary Peak

CALIFORNIA

Elevation

Feet	Meters
11,000	3,353
9,000	2,743
7,000	2,134
5,000	1,524
3,000	914
1,000	305

N W E S

0   50 Miles
0   50 Kilometers

Las Vegas

Lake Mead

Henderson

Boulder City

Colorado

ARIZONA

such as the Walker River, which flows into Walker Lake. Most rivers flow into sinks, low-lying areas that may collect water during rainy seasons. When the water evaporates, it leaves flat, sun-baked lake beds. The Humboldt River is the longest river in the Great Basin and Nevada's longest river. It runs westward across northern Nevada, ending in Humboldt Sink.

Pyramid Lake was once part of Lake Lahontan. But over the years, much of the water of the larger lake evaporated.

WORD TO KNOW

evaporated *dried up*

The waters of a few Nevada rivers do leave the state. The Muddy River and the Virgin River flow southward into the Colorado River.

Thousands of years ago, northwest Nevada lay underwater. An ancient inland lake called Lake Lahontan covered much of northern Nevada. As the centuries passed, most of the water **evaporated**. Today, all that's left of Lake Lahontan are Pyramid Lake and Walker Lake. Pyramid Lake is the largest natural lake that lies entirely within the state.

At the southern tip of the state, Lake Mead forms part of the border between Nevada and Arizona. It's an artificial lake created by Hoover Dam on the Colorado River. Other small lakes lie high in Nevada's many mountain ranges.

More than 160 mountain ranges run through Nevada. They were created millions of years ago as

Earth's crust shifted and thrust up massive chunks of rock. Hot springs and occasional earthquakes are evidence that, even today, the land is still shifting.

Most of Nevada's Great Basin mountain ranges run in a north–south direction through the state. They include the Ruby Mountains in the east; Shoshone, Toiyabe, and Toquima mountains in central Nevada; and the Spring Mountains in the south. In the White Mountains, to the southwest, is Boundary Peak. Broad valleys spread out among Nevada's mountain ranges. Some valleys are grassy ranges where cattle graze. Others are deserts or dry lake beds.

Mojave Desert

Drive through Nevada, and you'll see a lot of dry, dusty, or sandy soil. Much of northern Nevada lies within the Great Basin Desert. Southern Nevada is lower, hotter, and drier. Its southern tip is covered by the Mojave Desert, where short mountain ranges punctuate wide plains.

The Columbia Plateau

In the northeastern part of Nevada, a very small section along the Idaho border lies within the Columbia Plateau. This plateau extends northward into neighboring Oregon and Idaho. Its rivers and streams run through deep, rugged canyons. Nevada's Owyhee and other rivers flow northward into Idaho's Snake River.

Sierra Nevada

Named for the Sierra Nevada mountain range, the Sierra Nevada region is even smaller than the part of Nevada in the Columbia Plateau. It rises on Nevada's western border with California. Most of the Sierra

SEE IT HERE!

GREAT BASIN NATIONAL PARK

Great Basin National Park lies in eastern Nevada, near Baker and the Utah border. Within the park is rugged Wheeler Peak, Nevada's second-highest point. At the base of the mountain are Lehman Caves, whose winding passageways lead visitors past amazing rock formations. Higher up the mountain are groves of ancient bristlecone pines.

Many different kinds of animals live in the park. They include mountain lions, bobcats, and coyotes. Jackrabbits, ground squirrels, mule deer, and antelope range across the lowlands, while bighorn sheep move nimbly along the rocky mountain slopes.

Great Basin National Park was established in 1986 and it covers about 120 square miles (311 sq km).

A NOBLE SHEET OF BLUE WATER

Writer Mark Twain saw Lake Tahoe while traveling through Nevada in 1861. Here's how he described his first view of the lake:

"At last the Lake burst upon us—a noble sheet of blue water lifted six thousand three hundred feet above the level of the sea, and walled in by a rim of snow-clad mountain peaks that towered aloft a full three thousand feet higher still! . . . As it lay there with the shadows of the mountains brilliantly photographed upon its still surface[,] I thought it must surely be the fairest picture the whole earth affords."

Nevada range is in California. In Nevada, its granite peaks rise abruptly from the flat desert landscape. Some of these peaks are snowcapped year-round. The snowy mountaintops overlook beautiful Lake Tahoe, which straddles both California and Nevada. Lake Tahoe is the second-deepest lake in the United States. Only Oregon's Crater Lake is deeper. For the Washoe people who once inhabited this area, Lake Tahoe was the center of their culture.

Three major rivers start in the Sierra Nevada and end in the Great Basin: the Truckee River, which empties into Pyramid Lake, the Carson River, which empties into Carson Sink, and the Walker River.

A skier admires the majestic beauty of Lake Tahoe in the winter.

Weather Report

This chart shows record temperatures (high and low) for the state, as well as average temperatures (January and July) and average annual precipitation.

Record high temperature . . . . 125°F (52°C) at Laughlin
. . . . on June 29, 1994
Record low temperature . . . . –50°F (–46°C) at San Jacinto
. . . . on January 8, 1937
Average temperature in January, Las Vegas . . . . . . 49°F (9°C)
Average temperature in July, Las Vegas . . . . 93°F (34°C)
Average yearly precipitation, Las Vegas . . 4.2 inches (10.7 cm)

Source: National Climatic Data Center, NESDIS, NOAA, U.S. Department of Commerce

CLIMATE

Nevada lies in what's called the rain shadow of the Sierra Nevada. These high mountains block moisture-bearing storm clouds that drift eastward from the Pacific Ocean, so that Nevada gets an average of only a few inches of **precipitation** every year. It's the driest state in the entire United States.

Storms

As in other desert regions, daytime temperatures drop sharply once the sun goes down. Some storms do break past the Sierra Nevada mountains. Sudden thunderstorms can blow in and drench an area, then move on just as quickly. The Sierra Nevada and the Lake Tahoe area get the most rainfall. Most of the state's snow falls high in these mountains. Occasionally, the weather in these high altitudes will get so cold that incoming storms over the Sierra Nevada bring devastating blizzards. Northern Nevada and the mountainous regions have long, cold winters and short, hot summers. In the north, the average January temperature is 24 degrees

WORD TO KNOW

precipitation *cloud-borne moisture such as rain and snow*

The U.S. government manages about 85 percent of Nevada's land—more than 60 million acres (24 million hectares)! No other state has so much government-managed land.

This parched land is part of the Mojave Desert. Temperatures on valley floors and dry lake beds can soar above 120°F (49°C) and above 130°F (54°C) at the lowest elevations.

Fahrenheit (–4 degrees Celsius). Winters are not as bitterly cold in the western part of the state, though the summers are hot.

Droughts

Southern and west-central Nevada are the driest parts of the state. Southern Nevada is the hottest region. Even in January, the average temperature there is 43°F (6°C). But in July, the average is above 90°F (32°C). During summer months, there are periods when it might not rain for weeks. Little moisture, coupled with the intense heat, give way to droughts so severe that the earth begins to crack! One of the state government's top priorities is to figure out how to solve the water problems in these drier areas to prevent future droughts from occurring.

PLANT LIFE

Gaze across Nevada's desert landscapes, from the Great Basin high desert to the Mojave Desert in the south, and you'll see many hardy, dry-weather plants. Chances

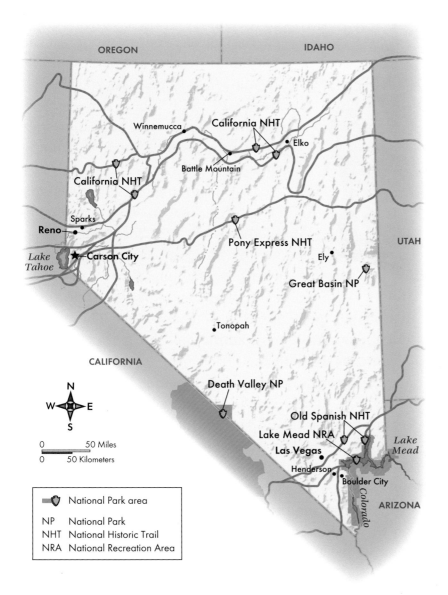

Nevada National Park Areas

This map shows some of Nevada's national parks, monuments, preserves, and other areas protected by the National Park Service.

OREGON

IDAHO

Winnemucca

California NHT

Elko

California NHT

Battle Mountain

California NHT

Sparks

Reno

Pony Express NHT

UTAH

Lake Tahoe

Carson City

Ely

Great Basin NP

Tonopah

CALIFORNIA

N
W E
S

0   50 Miles
0   50 Kilometers

Death Valley NP

Old Spanish NHT

Lake Mead NRA

Lake Mead

Las Vegas

Henderson

Boulder City

Colorado

ARIZONA

National Park area

NP   National Park
NHT   National Historic Trail
NRA   National Recreation Area

are, you'll see plenty of low bushes with silvery green leaves. These are sagebrush plants. Sagebrush is so widespread across the state that one of Nevada's nicknames is the Sagebrush State. The sagebrush's tiny yellow blossoms are the state flower.

A cross-country skier admires an ancient bristlecone pine near Wheeler Peak.

WORD TO KNOW

staple *basic, essential*

Pine nuts contain more protein than any other nut or seed in the world!

Other desert plants include cactus, yucca, and mesquite. In the mountains and valleys are grassy meadows that provide splashes of color when they bloom in the spring. Tough grasses such as Indian rice grass provide food for both wildlife and grazing cattle.

Although much of Nevada is very dry, forests cover about 15 percent of the state. Most forest trees grow on the mountainsides. There you'll find pine, fir, and juniper trees. The piñon (or pinyon) pine is one of Nevada's state trees. It's known for its seeds, called pine nuts. These tasty, nutritious nuts were a **staple** food for Nevada's Native Americans for thousands of years.

Nevada's other state tree is the amazing bristlecone pine. These trees are the oldest living things on the planet. They can live more than 4,000 years! Some of Nevada's bristlecone pines were already growing when ancient Egyptians were building the great pyramids! Bristlecone pines, with their gnarly, twisted trunks, grow high in the mountains. They can be found on the higher reaches of the Spring Mountains, Ruby Mountains, and other ranges, and on Wheeler Peak.

ANIMAL LIFE

Gigantic creatures once lived in Nevada. Massive mammoths roamed the land, and other creatures swam in the ancient seas. Today, Nevada's animals are much smaller. Desert bighorn sheep inhabit rocky canyons and mountainsides. They are Nevada's state animal. Mule deer are found throughout much of the state. Pronghorns, which are similar to antelope, graze in the broad valleys between mountain ranges. Pronghorns can run faster than any other hoofed animal in North America. Some have been known to reach 60 miles (97 km) an hour! The state also boasts a number of elk herds, as well as a growing population of mountain goats.

Many small animals scurry across Nevada's desert landscape. The badger is quite common, as are coyotes, foxes, porcupines, ground squirrels, rabbits, and kangaroo rats. The kangaroo rat can live its whole life without drinking water! It has a process of making water within its own body by converting the dry seeds it eats into water. Kangaroo rats neither sweat nor pant like other animals to keep cool. They also have specialized kidneys that allow them to dispose of bodily waste with very little output of water. Lizards, Gila monsters, and rattlesnakes live in the desert, too. To escape the heat, many of these animals are nocturnal. That means they sleep in the day, becoming only active at night.

A bighorn sheep

WHEELER PEAK PINE

Imagine finding the oldest bristlecone pine on Earth—and then cutting it down! That's what a university student may have done. In 1964, he was doing research on bristlecone pines on Nevada's Wheeler Peak. He found one that was especially interesting and, with permission from the U.S. Forest Service, cut it down to study it. By counting the rings in the trunk, scientists found that it was more than 4,900 years old. Ring-counting is a tricky business, though. Some scientists believe the tree may have been at least 5,000 years old. That would make it the oldest organism ever known.

The Wheeler Peak pine was named Prometheus, after a figure from ancient Greek mythology. It was Prometheus who stole fire from the gods and gave it to humans. The good news is that the Prometheus incident led to increased security measures to protect bristlecone pines, including the creation of Great Basin National Park.

SEE IT HERE!

BERLIN-ICHTHYOSAUR STATE PARK

Ichthyosaurs were giant prehistoric reptiles shaped sort of like dolphins. They lived about 225 million years ago. The largest ichthyosaur fossil ever known was discovered in what is now Berlin-Ichthyosaur State Park near Gabbs. It's 55 feet (17 meters) long! Nevada is the only state that has a complete ichthyosaur skeleton.

Ichthyosaurs first appeared about 250 million years ago. They swam in the shallow sea that once covered much of Nevada, and their huge eyes helped them find food in the dark waters. Fossils of about 40 ichthyosaurs were found in this area, which contains North America's largest concentration of ichthyosaur fossils. Visitors can see them, as well as watch scientists at work on the dig sites.

Two Nevada fish are found nowhere else on Earth. The cui-ui lives only in Pyramid Lake, and the Devils Hole pupfish lives only in Devils Hole!

Cactus wrens and roadrunners are some of Nevada's desert birds. Ducks, geese, and other waterbirds nest around lakes and streams. Other Nevada birds include eagles, hawks, owls, and grouse. Anahoe Island Refuge, in Pyramid Lake, is a nesting place for hundreds of white pelicans.

Nevada is home to more than half the mustangs, or wild horses, in the United States. Burros run wild in Nevada, too. A burro is about half the size of a horse, and it has long ears. Mustang and burro herds are protected in dozens of areas throughout the state. One is the Nevada Wild Horse Range. It lies within Nellis Air Force Base, northeast of Las Vegas. The Marietta Wild Burro Range is in western Nevada, near Mina.

ENDANGERED SPECIES

While many animals adapt to the harsh conditions of the desert areas, some animals cannot. Today, according to the Nevada Department of Conservation and Natural Resources, there are 26 plant, insect, fish, and bird species on the endangered list. Endangered Nevada plant life includes the Steamboat buckwheat and the Amargosa niterwart. The sole endangered insect in Nevada is the Carson wandering skipper. Endangered fish include the cui-ui, woundfin, Independence Valley speckled dace, and the razorback sucker. Endangered birds include the Yuma clapper rail and the southwestern willow flycatcher. For most of them, the struggle has not been because of Nevada's harsh desert conditions, but because of the ever-increasing expansion of its cities.

ENVIRONMENTAL ISSUES

Issues such as the water crisis and the fate of the state's endangered species will not be resolved overnight. It will take the effort of everyone, both in the state of Nevada and nationally, to solve these problems. The people of Nevada are educating themselves about the environmental issues that the state is currently facing. They know it's up to them to keep the air clean, the land plentiful, and the wildlife prosperous!

VELMA BRONN JOHNSTON: SAVING THE MUSTANGS

Nicknamed Wild Horse Annie, Velma Bronn Johnston (1912–1977) was a tireless crusader for Nevada's wild horses. She was horrified to see people kill the horses for sale to pet food plants and even shoot them just for sport. As a result of these activities, the wild horse population was shrinking dramatically. So Johnson began a public-awareness campaign, recruiting Nevada schoolkids to take an active part. These efforts led to the passage of the Wild Free-Roaming Horses and Burros Act of 1971. It protected these animals from harassment on public lands.

? Want to know more? Visit www.factsfornow .scholastic.com and enter the keyword **Nevada**.

Wild horses in Nevada's Amargosa Desert

READ ABOUT

Ancient peoples created petroglyphs, carvings like these at Valley of Fire State Park. These petroglyphs have dated human life in the region somewhere between 300 BCE and 1150 CE.

9000 BCE

The first humans arrive in Nevada

c. 7400 BCE

Spirit Cave Man lives near Fallon

▲ 1000 BCE

The Northern Paiute live along Pyramid Lake

CHAPTER TWO

FIRST PEOPLE

★

THOUSANDS AND THOUSANDS OF YEARS AGO, PEOPLE CARVED PICTURES AND OTHER DESIGNS ON CLIFFS AND ROCK SURFACES IN THE REGION THAT IS NOW NEVADA. Scientists and archaeologists today are trying to unlock the puzzles hidden in these pictures, called petroglyphs. They are keys to an ancient way of life—a rich culture whose secrets are still unfolding.

1100

Paiute create petroglyphs at Red Rock

1500s ▸
A thriving community exists at Winnemucca Lake

1800s ▸
White settlers enter Native American homelands

WORD TO KNOW

archaeologists *scientists who study the remains of human cultures*

SEE IT HERE!

Among Nevada's many petroglyph sites are Grimes Point, near Fallon; Hickison Summit, near Austin; Red Rock Canyon, west of Las Vegas; and Valley of Fire State Park, northeast of Las Vegas.

A Southern Paiute arrow maker and a child, near the Colorado River Valley. The Southern Paiute Indians dominated the southern part of what is now Nevada.

EARLY LIFE

Anthropologists and **archaeologists** are beginning to piece together the Native American legends and stories of the creation and origin of their people. One legend is typical of many groups. It tells the story of Tawa, the Sun God, and Spider Woman, the Earth Goddess. No living thing existed until these two willed it to be. First they willed Earth's land formations. Then they willed the birds, fish, beasts, and finally the earliest Native tribes who would rule over the newly created land. This was the creation of the world.

Many scholars believe that the first humans arrived in Nevada about 11,000 years ago. They were descendants of people who crossed over a strip of land that once connected northeast Asia to the northwest Americas. They were following herds of large **game** animals. They hunted mastodons, musk oxen, mammoths, bison, giant ground sloths, and even camels. Nevada's early people also gathered plants for food. In **prehistoric** Lake Lahontan, they caught abundant fish.

Winnemucca Lake, now dry, became a center for thriving cultures. In Lovelock Cave, archaeologists have found objects that people made as early as 4,700 years ago. They include duck **decoys**, stone and bone tools, and woven textiles, as well as beads, pendants, and other ornaments. Bird bones, plant seeds, and even scorpion stingers were made into ornaments, too. We know these people traded with other groups because some ornaments were made with seashells from the Pacific Ocean, hundreds of miles to the west.

As Nevada's climate grew hotter and drier, the large game animals died out. Lake Lahontan receded, leaving Pyramid Lake and Walker Lake behind. As their environment changed, Nevada's people changed their way of life. They clustered in family groups that moved from place to place as the seasons changed. Usually they lived in one spot during the summer and moved to a more sheltered place for the winter. At each new location, they built homes out of materials they found in the area, such as branches, bark, reeds, and grasses. Some people lived in caves. Because of the arid climate, few groups farmed, but they were very good at hunting and gathering plants.

Eventually, four main Native American groups developed in Nevada—the Washoe, Northern Paiute, Southern Paiute, and Western Shoshone. They belong to what are called the Great Basin groups.

WORDS TO KNOW

game *animals hunted for food*

prehistoric *period before written or recorded history*

decoys *models of animals used to lure live animals for hunting*

SPIRIT CAVE MAN

This ancient man lived more than 9,400 years ago. Buried in a rabbit-skin robe and fur moccasins, he was surrounded by elaborate basketry. In 1940, his remains were discovered in Spirit Cave, near Fallon. He is called Spirit Cave Man. Who was he? And what background did he have? Scientists want to continue performing tests on the remains and artifacts. However, the Fallon Northern Paiute and Western Shoshone groups want Spirit Cave Man returned to his ancestral burial place so he can continue his spiritual journey. As of 2013, this controversy was still unresolved.

Native American Peoples

(Before European Contact)

This map shows the general area of Native American people before European settlers arrived.

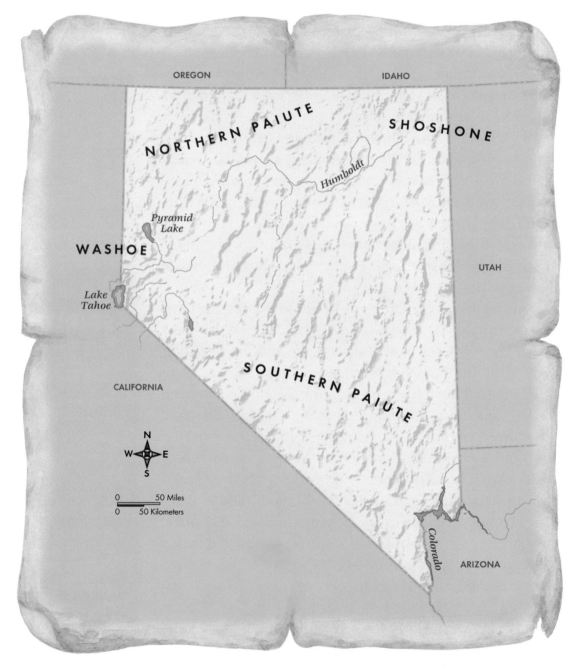

THE WASHOE

For an estimated 9,000 years, Nevada's Washoe people have made Lake Tahoe their cultural and spiritual center. Their traditional territory lay along the shores of Lake Tahoe and Washoe Lake and in the low-lying valleys of the eastern Sierras. During the winter, Washoe families settled in the Carson, Washoe, Truckee, and Walker river valleys. They built homes in a circle, with each home adjoining the next one, and made them with wooden poles covered with bark, thatched grasses, or deer hides.

In the late spring, the Washoe packed their belongings and moved to the banks of Lake Tahoe, where they built their summer camps. They made houses of reeds or brush woven with willow strips. From the lakeshore, the Washoe hunted ducks and mud hens and fished for trout. They sent out scouting parties to find areas where other wild game—mule deer, antelope, and rabbits—was abundant.

REDHEADED GIANTS

Paiute legends tell of fearsome, redheaded giants called the Saiduka, who kidnapped, killed, and sometimes even ate their neighbors. Mummies discovered in Lovelock Cave had red hair and stood as much as 7 feet (213 centimeters) tall! Could these be the people of the legends?

Basket weaving is a popular craft among the Washoe. A Washoe basket maker works outside her home, which is made of dried mud and sticks.

MINI-BIO

DAT-SO-LA-LEE: STORYTELLING BY DESIGN

Dat-So-La-Lee (c. 1829–1925) was a Washoe basket maker known for her excellent work, using designs to tell a story. Born near the mining town of Sheridan, she washed and cooked for mining families. She collected various plant materials for making her baskets. Then she wove them using ancient Washoe techniques and designs. She is best known for her degikup baskets, which had a small base, a wide body, and a small opening at the top.

? Want to know more? Visit www.factsfornow.scholastic.com and enter the keyword **Nevada**.

Q8 HOW DID LAKE TAHOE GET ITS NAME?

A8 The Washoe called the Lake Tahoe area Da-ow-a-ga, which means "edge of the lake." Pioneers misunderstood this word, interpreting the first two syllables as "Tahoe."

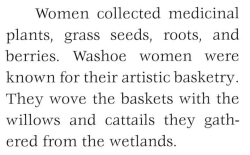

Women collected medicinal plants, grass seeds, roots, and berries. Washoe women were known for their artistic basketry. They wove the baskets with the willows and cattails they gathered from the wetlands.

In the autumn, the Washoe moved east to the Pine Nut Mountains, whose slopes were covered with piñon pine trees. There the Washoe women spent several weeks collecting pine nuts, the tasty seeds beneath the scales of the pinecone.

Each autumn, the Washoe began the pinecone-harvesting season, with a five-day ceremony to give thanks to the Maker (another word for God or Creator) for the harvest. Then men knocked the pinecones from the trees using a hooked pole. Women and children gathered the fallen cones and carried them back to camp in large baskets. When roasted over a fire, the cones burst open, making it easier to remove the nuts. The Washoe stored much of the nut harvest as a staple food for the winter. Women ground the nuts into a flour, which they combined with other ingredients and made into soup.

THE NORTHERN PAIUTE

The Northern Paiute lived across much of western Nevada, primarily on the shores of Pyramid Lake and Walker Lake. The lakeside marshes provided a wealth of food, such as fish and ducks, and useful materials,

Native Americans fished for cui-ui. And they made jerky from meat. Here cui-ui and jerky are drying out for later use.

such as cattails and **tule**. The Paiute would use cattail and tule not only as a nutritious food source, but also as thatch for their shelters.

In the spring, men and boys hunted ducks, using decoys to lure them. Those who lived around Pyramid Lake fished for cui-ui. Along the shore, women and girls gathered ducks' eggs, marsh plants, and roots. Men also went out on hunting expeditions for pronghorn, jack-rabbits, ground squirrels, and other small game.

In summer, the Northern Paiute moved into open-air structures with a roof for shade. They caught fish and dried them to eat in winter. Women picked berries and gathered rice and seeds to grind into a coarse meal. As in Great Basin groups, women ground seeds by placing them on a large, flat stone called a *metate* (meh-TAH-tee) and grinding them with a small, rounded stone called a *mano* (MAH-noh).

WORD TO KNOW

tule *a flexible, thick-stemmed marsh plant*

Picture Yourself . . .

Making a Tule Duck Decoy

Suppose you are a Northern Paiute. You are living on the shore of Pyramid Lake 3,000 years ago. Springtime is here, and you need to make a decoy for duck hunting. Beside the lake, you scan the marshy banks for water plants. You gather an armload of long, thick-stemmed tules and strip leaves off some cattails.

Back at camp, you soak the cattail leaves in water and twist them into a twine. Next, you bend the tules in half, tying the bent center with cattail twine. This will be the decoy's front end. With your flint knife, you trim the rear end so it points upward. This will be the decoy's tail. Now you hollow out the tule bundle, shaping it into the form of a duck's body. On the front, you use more tule to shape a neck and head. All that's left is to tie the bill shut. Your decoy is ready to set afloat!

WORDS TO KNOW

tributaries *smaller rivers that flow into a larger river*

chaff *husks of grains, corn or other seeds that have been chopped off of their hulls*

winnowing *a method of separating grains from their hulls*

In the fall, they gathered pine nuts in the mountains where piñon pine trees grew. Fall was also the time for rabbit drives, or group rabbit-hunting expeditions. In the winter, the Northern Paiute built homes that were partly underground. They were made of poles covered with branches, grasses, and soil. Winter was a time for making new tools and clothes. It was also a time to gather around the fire for evenings of storytelling.

THE SOUTHERN PAIUTE

The Southern Paiute lived mainly in southern Nevada. Some settled around the springs of the Las Vegas Valley or the nearby Spring Mountains. (These mountains are named for their many freshwater springs.) Others gathered near the Colorado River and its **tributaries**.

In summer, they used willow and brush to build shelters that served as shade and as a windbreak. Using bows and arrows, they hunted big game such as deer, antelope, and mountain sheep. They dried both the meat and the hides for later use. To catch small game, they used nets or clubs. Women picked berries, mesquite beans, and other plants to round out their diet.

In the fall, the Southern Paiute gathered pine nuts, sunflowers, and various seeds. To separate seeds from the **chaff**, women used special trays. When they tossed the grains in the air, the wind carried the lightweight chaff away, while the tender, heavier seeds landed back in the **winnowing** tray. Autumn was also the time to make sure there was enough food to last through winter. People stored food in safe places such as caves.

In winter, the Southern Paiute made their homes in caves or dirt-covered shelters, they then turned their attention to indoor projects. People tanned deer, antelope, and rabbit hides to make warm clothes and shoes. Sagebrush and grass were made into shirts, skirts, and leggings. Women wove lightweight basketry from grass, willow, and bark. Woven items included beds for babies, large baskets for household goods, and winnowing trays. Winter was also a time for storytelling and singing traditional songs.

A Northern Pauite woman demonstrates how pine nuts were traditionally cleaned before use.

EARLY FARMERS

Like other Great Basin peoples, the Southern Paiute were hunter-gatherers. However, those who lived near rivers and springs also practiced some farming. They dug ditches for **irrigation** and raised corn, squash, melons, gourds, and sunflowers.

WORD TO KNOW

irrigation *a method of channeling water from rivers or lakes to farmland*

The Western Shoshone people primarily settled in the eastern part of the state.

HEALING PLANTS

The Southern Paiute used many herbs from the Spring Mountains as medicines. Usually they boiled the plant to make a tea for the sick person to drink. Angelica root helped stomachaches and colds. Milkvetch and eggvetch relieved toothaches and other pains. Greasebrush was prescribed for tuberculosis. Beardtongue species helped sores, burns, itches, and other skin problems. These are just a few of the dozens of medicinal plants the Southern Paiute knew how to use. Some people still use many of these herbal remedies to treat common sicknesses.

THE WESTERN SHOSHONE

The Western Shoshone lived in the eastern half of Nevada. In spring, they cut limbs from the choke-cherry to make hunting bows. They chipped bone, flint, or obsidian to make arrow points. These were used to hunt groundhogs, ground squirrels, and sage hens. The Shoshone also made traps and nets to catch small animals. They sharpened sticks to make digging tools to unearth wild onions, sego and camas roots, and wild asparagus and carrots. They knew which plants to use as medicines, too. Various plants could treat sores, colds, and other illnesses.

In summer, Shoshone families camped in the mountains. There they used spears, nets, and willow traps to catch salmon and trout in the cool mountain streams. Using poisoned arrows or spear tips, they hunted for big game such as deer and bighorn sheep.

In fall, they gathered ripe currants and other berries. They also gathered pine nuts and ground them into flour, which they then made into soup or gravy. Fewer edible plants grew at this time of year, so meat became an important food supply. On group hunting drives, they hunted antelope, deer, and rabbits. The meat belonged to the group and was divided among all the families. As winter was coming on, some of the meat was made into jerky. They also cured the hides to use later. Rabbits were especially valuable now. They had grown their thick winter coats, which were sewn together to make rabbit-skin blankets.

When winter came, the Shoshone moved to permanent winter home sites. Through the long winter, they gathered around the fires and listened to storytellers, just as neighboring groups did. Their tales, passed down for generations, revealed Shoshone history and traditional legends. Animals—especially the clever coyote—were the main characters in many of the legends.

In the 1800s, non-Native Americans began to enter the Indians' homelands. Traditional hunting grounds became busy trails for pioneers and those seeking their fortune in the West. For Nevada's Indians, life would never be the same again.

COYOTE, THE ANIMAL SPIRIT

For the Western Shoshone and Northern Paiute, Coyote was a powerful animal spirit. He and his bride had a great number of children, and he stored them in a willow jug. These children were the forefathers of all Indian groups. They all escaped and scattered, except for two, whom Coyote released in the Great Basin. They were the forefathers of the Western Shoshone and the Northern Paiute.

SARAH WINNEMUCCA: PAIUTE PEACEMAKER

Her original name was Thocmetony, meaning "shell flower." But as the daughter of Paiute chief Winnemucca, she became known as Sarah Winnemucca (c. 1844–1891). She believed in making peace with whites. After learning English and Spanish, she worked as an interpreter and scout for the U.S. Army. She also traveled to Washington, D.C., to attempt to gain support for her people. Her book, Life Among the Paiutes: Their Wrongs and Claims (1883), is still read today.

? Want to know more? Visit www.factsfornow.scholastic.com and enter the keyword **Nevada**.

READ ABOUT

An early silver mine in Nevada. Silver proved to be an economic success for the territory.

1776

A Spanish priest is the first European to enter Nevada

1821

Nevada comes under Mexican control

▲**1826**

Trappers Peter Skene Ogden and Jedediah Smith (above) explore Nevada

CHAPTER THREE

EXPLORATION AND SETTLEMENT

★

BEGINNING IN THE LATE 1700S, MISSIONARIES, ADVENTURERS, AND COVERED WAGONS FULL OF PIONEERS MADE THEIR WAY INTO NEVADA. The first European to arrive was Francisco Garcés in 1776. This Franciscan priest was searching for a route from Tucson, Arizona, to California. He traveled alone, relying on Native Americans as guides.

1829

Mexican trader Antonio Armijo makes the first round-trip through Nevada

1843–1845

John C. Frémont and Kit Carson explore the region

▲1844

The Stephens-Townsend-Murphy party travels on the California Trail

Trappers discovering a beaver caught in one of their traps. In the early 1800s, beaver fur was in great demand for making hats and coats.

TRAPPERS AND TRAILS

The same year the priests entered Nevada, American colonists on the eastern seaboard issued their Declaration of Independence from Great Britain. Their 13 colonies would become the United States of America. But at the time, these faraway events were of little interest in Nevada.

In 1821, Mexico won independence from Spain. The land now called Nevada came under Mexican control. Around the same time, the thick fur of the beaver was in high demand for making hats and coats. Soon fur trappers from around the world were exploring the territory.

Trapper Peter Skene Ogden probably crossed into northeastern Nevada in 1826. Two years later, he discovered the Humboldt River as he crossed the Great Basin. On his way north to Oregon, Ogden reached the eastern face of the Sierra Nevada, where he also came upon the Carson and Owens lakes. Ogden's journeys into the American West would not go undocumented.

In 1853, a year before his death, he anonymously published a book about American Indian life entitled, *Traits of American-Indian Life and Character.*

Another trapper, Jedediah Smith, crossed southeastern Nevada in 1826 on his way to California, becoming the first non-Native person ever to enter California from the east. The next year, he crossed the Sierra Nevada from California and explored central Nevada. Smith and his team became the first Americans to return from California on an overland route across the Sierra Nevada.

THINK ABOUT IT!

U.S. Settlement of the West

PRO

Many European Americans were eager to expand across the whole North American continent and make settlements. They garnered support for their cause by claiming that God had given them the right to do so. As John O'Sullivan said in 1845: "[Other nations hamper] the fulfillment of our manifest destiny to overspread the continent allotted by Providence for the free development of our yearly multiplying millions."

CON

Native Americans had lived on their ancestral homelands for centuries. It was understood that each group respected the others' territories. So the Washoe of California and Nevada stated: "[Our land] was positioned directly in the path of explorers, immigrants, and gold-seekers. . . . The total occupation of the Washoe peoples' former lands took only a few short years."

Source: John O'Sullivan, "Annexation," *United States Magazine and Democratic Review 17*, no.1, July–August 1845; www.washoetribe.us

Exploration of Nevada

The colored arrows on this map show the routes taken by explorers and pioneers between 1776 and 1845.

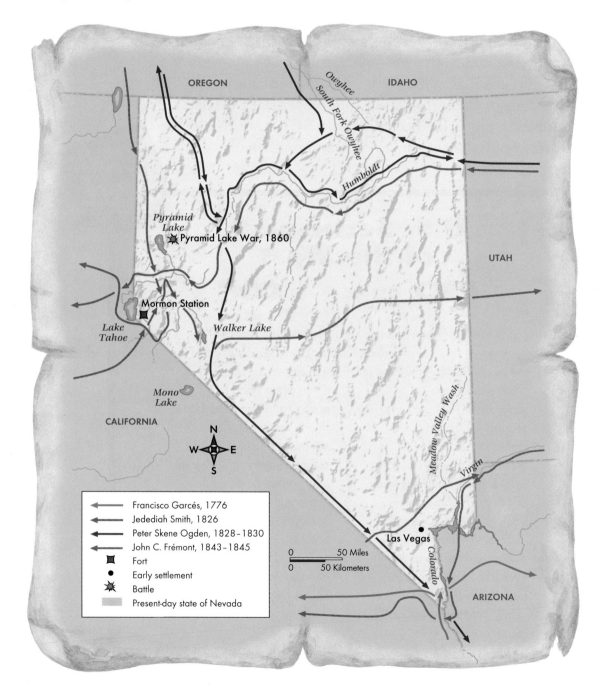

OREGON

IDAHO

Owyhee

South Fork Owyhee

Humboldt

UTAH

Pyramid Lake

✸ Pyramid Lake War, 1860

Mormon Station

Walker Lake

Lake Tahoe

Mono Lake

CALIFORNIA

N
W   E
S

Meadow Valley Wash

Virgin

Las Vegas

Colorado

Francisco Garcés, 1776
Jedediah Smith, 1826
Peter Skene Ogden, 1828–1830
John C. Frémont, 1843–1845
🛡 Fort
● Early settlement
✸ Battle
    Present-day state of Nevada

0   50 Miles
0   50 Kilometers

ARIZONA

Explorers and traders began blazing trails through the territory. These trails ran through mountains, deserts, and canyons. In 1829, Mexican trader Antonio Armijo marked out what came to be known as the Old Spanish Trail. It passed through southern Nevada on its way between Santa Fe, New Mexico, and Los Angeles, California. Mexican and American traders used it to transport woolen items, horses, and other trade goods.

PUSHING WESTWARD

In the 1840s, a new idea was taking hold in the United States. It was called manifest destiny. This was the belief that the United States had a mission to expand the

LOST BOY FINDS LAS VEGAS!

Antonio Armijo established the Old Spanish Trail, but he couldn't have done it without a lost boy. In 1829, Armijo set out to find a route between the territories of New Mexico and California. On Christmas Day, he set up camp in northwestern Arizona and sent out scouts to find the best route to take next. Among them was a teenager named Rafael Rivera. The scouts returned to camp, but where was Rivera? He had gotten lost. While he was wandering, he discovered a valley with bubbling springs and green meadows. This was the perfect route through the desert lands. After reuniting with Armijo's men, Rivera led them to the lush spot. They named the valley Las Vegas—Spanish for "the meadows."

MINI-BIO

TRUCKEE: REACHING OUT IN FRIENDSHIP

Truckee (?–1860) was a Northern Paiute chief. His Paiute name may have been Tru-ki-zo, later mispronounced by whites. Truckee believed all people had the same ancestor, and he welcomed his "white brothers." In 1843, he guided explorer John C. Frémont through the Great Basin and later fought under Frémont in the Mexican-American War. Truckee also showed the Stephens-Townsend-Murphy group of pioneers how to reach the river that would take them safely through the Sierra Nevada. That river was named the Truckee River in his honor.

? Want to know more? Visit www.factsfornow.scholastic.com and enter the keyword **Nevada**.

Kit Carson and his team of snow dogs. Carson served as a guide for explorer John C. Frémont.

country all the way to the Pacific Ocean. In the spirit of manifest destiny, army officer John C. Frémont led many expeditions through the West.

Native Americans helped Frémont find his way in the wilderness and pointed out the best routes to take. Indians also taught Frémont how to make snowshoes out of bark. This helped his men travel through snowy land in the winter. From 1843 to 1845, Frémont and his guide, Kit Carson, explored and mapped the Great Basin and the Sierra Nevada. As a young man, Carson had come to know the wilderness trails and the Native Americans of the West.

In northwestern Nevada, they reached a lake with a rocky, pyramid-shaped island in it. Frémont named the lake Pyramid Lake. In the winter of 1844, the two were the first white people to see Lake Tahoe. In his maps and journals, Frémont named the region the Great Basin. Frémont's reports proved very useful for later travelers.

THE FIRST CROSSING

In 1844, 10 families set out from Iowa in a wagon train, headed for a better life in California. This group of pioneers was called the Stephens-Townsend-Murphy party. Its captain was Elisha Stephens, who had spent years as a trapper in the wilderness. Another member, Caleb Greenwood, had been a mountain man, too. Once the party reached Nevada, they followed the Humboldt River valley. But when the river petered out at Humboldt Sink, they had no idea where to go. Luckily, they ran into Paiute chief Truckee. He showed them how to reach what is now called the Truckee River, which led to a pass through the Sierra Nevada. Although 50 people had left Iowa, 52 reached Sacramento, California. Two babies had been born along the way.

This group was the first wagon train to cross the Sierra Nevada, along what would become known as the California Trail. Thousands of pioneers would take this route in the years to come. Though many were successful, some faced tragedy on the perilous trail. In 1846, heavy snows stranded the Donner party. During the winter, almost half the party died of cold and starvation in the mountains.

As more and more Americans crossed the land claimed by Mexico, the United States and Mexico began clashing over land rights. In 1845, the United

Picture Yourself . . .

Crossing Nevada in a Wagon Train

Life on the trail was rough. Everyone, including children, had chores to do. If your family brought a cow along, you'd milk it every morning. Then you'd take a bucket down to the stream and bring back the day's drinking water. With the firewood you'd gathered, you'd help start the morning's fire. After breakfast, you'd help wash the dishes and pack up the wagon for another day on the trail. As the wagon rumbled along, you'd run ahead and clear stones and branches out of the way. If the trail was muddy, you'd lay brush and branches over the mud so the wagon wheels wouldn't sink in and get stuck. When it was time to stop and eat, you'd go fishing or hunting to get fresh meat. All these tasks helped keep the whole group moving along. Hardships endured on the trail made a new and better life in California that much sweeter.

The slopes of the Sierra Nevada were so steep that pioneers had to lower their wagons down the cliffs by ropes!

WORDS TO KNOW

annexed *took control of another territory or country by force*

boomtowns *towns that spring up quickly, often because of a mineral discovery*

States **annexed** what is now Texas from the Mexican territories, and claimed it as its own. These conflicts led to the Mexican War (1846–1848). Many of the battles in the war were fought south of the Rio Grande, as the U.S. military pushed the Mexican forces back deep into their own territory. On September 14, 1847, U.S. forces entered Mexico City, the capital of Mexico, and ended the war for good. Mexico lost, and much of the West and Southwest—including Nevada—became part of the United States. In 1850, Congress established the Utah Territory, which included most of present-day Nevada. The Utah Territory was part of the Compromise of 1850, which attempted to balance the interests between the slave states and Free States. The Utah Territory would later be divided, creating states such as Nevada and Colorado.

SETTLEMENTS AND FORTUNES

With Nevada under American control, after the Mexican War, people began making their way westward in droves. At the same time, many immigrants, mostly from Germany, Ireland, England, Italy, Switzerland, Poland, and Russia, began flooding into the United States looking for wealth, freedom, and a fresh start in a new world. Many of these immigrants, along with established American citizens, made the journey west to pioneer the new frontier. Even more travelers headed west to Oregon and California, as gold had been discovered there in 1848. Thousands of people flocked west, some hoping to strike it rich, others hoping to make a good living by providing goods and services to the miners in California's **boomtowns**. There was excitement in the air, and people could sense that opportunities awaited them out west.

Many pioneer routes that were taken through Nevada crossed Shoshone and Northern Paiute hunting grounds. At first, the Indians tried to simply ignore the trespassers. But as the numbers of wagon trains swelled, clashes began to break out. The pioneers' horses and cattle were destroying native crops. In Paiute and Washoe territory, pioneers were cutting down the precious piñon pines for fuel. To Nevada's Native Americans, the situation was clear: they had to fight for their very survival. There were many conflicts between the pioneers and the native people.

A pioneer family heading west. Many believed they could find better lives in Nevada and other territories.

JAMES "JIM" BECKWOURTH: AN AFRICAN AMERICAN MOUNTAIN MAN

Born as a slave to a white man and a woman of mixed race, James Beckwourth (1798–1866) was freed as a child and eventually signed on with a fur-trading expedition. While heading west, Beckwourth spent six years living among the Crow Indians. He returned to white settlements in 1833, after having learned much about the American Indian and the wilderness.

In April 1850, Beckwourth discovered a pass through the Sierra Nevada into California. Northwest of what is now Reno on Route 70, Beckwourth Pass became important to gold seekers traveling from eastern states.

? Want to know more? Visit www.factsfornow.scholastic.com and enter the keyword **Nevada**.

This was the site of one of the first non-Indian settlements in Nevada.

SEE IT HERE!

MORMON STATION STATE HISTORIC PARK

In Genoa, you'll see the rebuilt trading post and hotel that Mormon traders established in 1851. It was one of Nevada's first permanent white settlement. The trading post thrived by selling supplies to travelers bound for the California gold fields. It now houses a museum where you'll learn all about the settlement.

Westbound travelers needed supplies, so people set up temporary trading posts along the California Trail. In 1850, a group of Mormons (members of the Church of Jesus Christ of Latter-day Saints) from the Utah Territory built a makeshift trading post in the Carson Valley. Another group of Mormons came the next year and built a sturdier post and a hotel. Called Mormon Station (now Genoa), this was one of the first non-Indian settlements in Nevada. Other pioneers, both Mormon and non-Mormon, settled around the post.

Mormons settled other spots in Nevada, too. In 1855, a group of Mormon missionaries moved into the Las Vegas Valley. Their goals were to spread their religion to the Southern Paiute and teach them how to farm. They also sold goods and supplies to travelers along the Old Spanish Trail. The Mormons built an adobe fort by Las Vegas Creek and farmed the area using irrigation. Here, too, they were the first non-Indians to settle the area. The newcomers destroyed the Paiute's traditional lifestyle and spread diseases that killed much of the Paiute population.

For a decade, fortune hunters saw Nevada as just a place to cross on the way to California's riches. That was soon to change. When miners discovered silver in the western hills, Nevada itself would become a fortune hunter's paradise.

MINI-BIO

JOHN A. THOMPSON: HERE COMES SNOWSHOE!

When the skier came swooshing down Genoa Peak, people dropped everything and ran to meet him. It was "Snowshoe" Thompson! Born in Norway as Jon Torsteinson-Rue, he later changed his name to John A. Thompson (c. 1827–1876). People called him Snowshoe because he traveled on a pair of homemade, ski-shaped snowshoes. For 20 years (1856–1876), Thompson carried mail, medicine, and other supplies over the Sierra Nevada from Placerville, California, to Mormon Station, Nevada.

? **Want to know more?** Visit www.factsfornow.scholastic.com and enter the keyword **Nevada**.

The Comstock Lode was the first major U.S. deposit of silver ore. Here diggers ready themselves to dig deep tunnels to find more silver deposits, in the late 1800s.

1859

Silver is discovered near
Virginia City

1861

Congress creates the
Nevada Territory

▲ **1864**

Nevada becomes the
36th U.S. state

GROWTH AND CHANGE

CHAPTER FOUR

GROWTH AND CHANGE

★

R AGGED TENTS, RICKETY SHACKS, AND PILES OF RUBBLE COVERED THE HILLSIDES. Dirt-smudged men, armed with picks and shovels, swarmed over the land, their eyes blazing with anticipation. This was the scene in western Nevada after silver was discovered there. In 1859, prospectors came across the richest silver deposit in the nation.

◄ 1868
The Transcontinental Railroad opens

1857
The price of silver begins to fall, causing many Nevada mines to close

1907
The Newlands Irrigation Project is completed

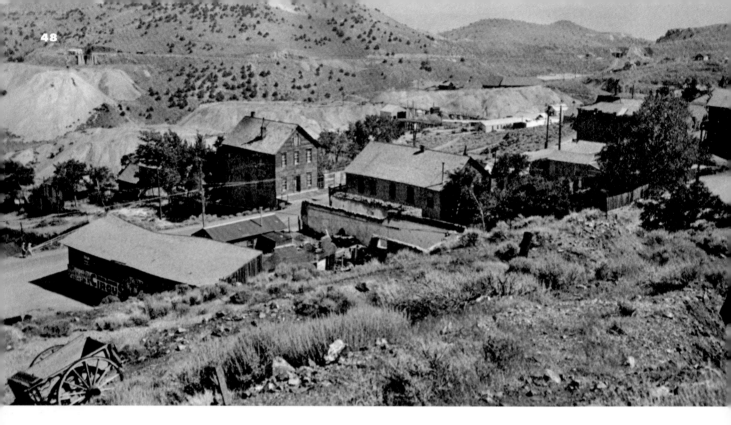

A view of Virginia City. This town was founded around the site where the Comstock Lode was discovered.

Between 1859 and 1878, the Comstock Lode yielded about $400 million worth of silver and gold. At today's prices, that would be more than $5 billion!

BOOMTOWN BLUES

There are several versions of the silver story. According to one, Patrick McLaughlin and Peter O'Reilly were looking for gold when they stumbled upon a rich vein of silver. While they were working, Henry Comstock came along. He declared that the land they were mining belonged to him. The two miners didn't want to cause any trouble, so they gave Comstock a share of their claim. This dazzling treasure was named the Comstock Lode, after the man who claimed the land where it was found.

Almost overnight, Virginia City sprang up around the mine site. Nearby Silver City and Gold Hill became mining boomtowns, too. Fortune-hunting prospectors rushed in from all over the world, as well as the United States. Many miners came from the mining regions of Wales and Cornwall, in southwest England. Immigrants from countries such as Ireland, Spain, Switzerland, Poland, and Russia came to these mining towns to try to get a share of the action. They scoured the hills and jammed into the boomtowns any way they could. At its peak, Virginia City swelled to about 30,000 people!

One newcomer to Virginia City was a writer named Samuel Langhorne Clemens. His brother, Orion Clemens, had been named territorial secretary when the Nevada Territory was established in 1861. When Samuel Clemens arrived in 1861, he took a job as a newspaper reporter for the *Territorial Enterprise.* Soon he began using the name for which he's best known—Mark Twain. He, too, was excited about the silver boom. In *Roughing It*, he wrote:

"Cart-loads of solid silver bricks, as large as pigs [castings] of lead, were arriving from the mills every day. . . . Almost every hour reveals new and more startling evidences of the profuse and intensified wealth of our favored county. . . . The intestines of our mountains are gorged with precious ore."

Twain lost a lot of money investing in mines. He wasn't the only one. Patrick McLaughlin eventually sold his share in the

W. H. C. STEPHENSON: THE ACTIVIST DOCTOR

When Nevada's silver rush was on, W. H. C. Stephenson (1825–c. 1873) moved to Virginia City. As a well-educated physician, he practiced medicine there, becoming Nevada's first African American doctor. Stephenson also became a prominent community leader in Virginia City. In the 1860s, he petitioned the Nevada legislature to grant blacks the right to testify in court cases. He also argued that, since blacks paid taxes, they should have equal access to public education.

? Want to know more? Visit www.factsfornow.scholastic.com and enter the keyword **Nevada**.

SEE IT HERE!

VIRGINIA CITY HISTORIC DISTRICT

The old mining boomtown of Virginia City is now a historic district. Stroll down the wooden sidewalks, and you'll pass dozens of saloons and general stores. Check out the Territorial Enterprise Building. That's where writer Mark Twain worked as a reporter. Today, the lower floor is a museum that includes Twain's old desk. Then stop by the Fourth Ward School, built in 1876. It's now a museum with changing exhibits. Or visit the Way It Was Museum to see mining equipment, photos, and maps. Piper's Opera House and the Nevada Gambling Museum are other great places to visit. For a first-class tour through the mining region, you can ride a steam train on the Virginia and Truckee Railroad. Or ride a tram through town on a narrated tour.

Many Basque sheepherders from California decided to move to Nevada. The land was good for raising sheep, and the demand for mutton was strong.

WORD TO KNOW

Basque *European people of ancient origin whose homeland is the Basque region of northeastern Spain and southwestern France*

Comstock Lode for $3,500. He lived in poverty for the rest of his life. Peter O'Reilly sold his share for $50,000. After several business ventures, he lost everything and went insane. Henry Comstock sold his share for $20,000. He then opened stores in Carson City and Silver City, but he eventually went broke. Next, he went prospecting in Idaho and Montana but found nothing. Totally dejected, he died in 1870.

Around this time **Basque** sheepherders in California were looking for new ranges for their sheep. They had been so successful in California that it was becoming too crowded. They began moving into Nevada, where the landscape was ideal for raising sheep and the market for mutton to feed the miners was strong. Ironically, these Basque sheepherders had gotten into the business after failing to strike it rich in the California gold rush.

Though some miners did get rich in Nevada, the real wealth went to those who formed big mining companies. Only big corporations could afford to buy the expensive equipment needed for large-scale mining operations.

THE BATTLE BORN STATE

Since 1850, Nevada had been part of Utah Territory. Now it was ready to become a territory of its own, owing to its rapid growth and expansion from the prospectors coming to Virginia City in search of silver and gold. In 1861, Congress created the Nevada Territory, with Carson City as its capital.

While the silver boom was going on, the United States was locked in the Civil War (1861–1865). Northern and Southern states were fighting this war over slavery. President Abraham Lincoln wanted another Free (non-slave) State in the Union. Thus, Nevada was admitted as the 36th U.S. state on October 31, 1864. Nevada is sometimes called the Battle Born State because it gained statehood during the Civil War.

After the Civil War, Nevada quickly ratified the three constitutional amendments that ended slavery and extended full civil rights to former slaves. However, Nevada's legislature denied children of "Negroes, Mongolians, and Indians" admission to state schools. Black Nevadans began a campaign for equal educational rights. "We have several colored children here who are growing up in ignorance, all on account of the white man's prejudices," said Thomas Detter, a community leader. "I ask, when will 'man's inhumanity to man' cease?" In 1866, 16 black children were admitted to a Nevada school, and an evening school also opened its doors. But in Carson City, the African

Virginia City Historic District is one of the nation's largest National Historic Landmarks. More than 2 million people visit the site every year!

Nevada: From Territory to Statehood

This map shows the original Utah Territory (outlined in green) and the area (in yellow) that became the state of Nevada in 1864.

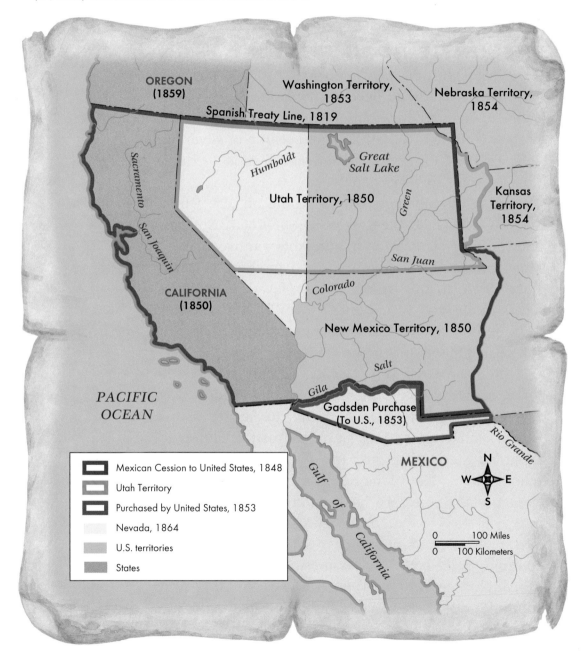

OREGON (1859)

Washington Territory, 1853

Nebraska Territory, 1854

Spanish Treaty Line, 1819

Sacramento

San Joaquin

Humboldt

Great Salt Lake

Green

Utah Territory, 1850

Kansas Territory, 1854

San Juan

CALIFORNIA (1850)

Colorado

New Mexico Territory, 1850

Salt

PACIFIC OCEAN

Gila

Gadsden Purchase (To U.S., 1853)

Rio Grande

MEXICO

N
W ✦ E
S

Gulf of California

	Mexican Cession to United States, 1848
	Utah Territory
	Purchased by United States, 1853
	Nevada, 1864
	U.S. territories
	States

0   100 Miles
0   100 Kilometers

American community had to raise $200 to build their own school. Parents said, "We value our black babies as well as other folks do theirs." Years of mounting protests persuaded the Elko County School Board to end segregation, and by 1880 most children of color attended state public schools.

In 1874, Nevada had only 396 African American citizens. Many lived in widely scattered communities. To combat loneliness, black women in Virginia City and Carson City organized literary discussions clubs to promote social relations and adult education. Some black women became successful in business. In 1874, Anna Graham began a hairdressing salon on C Street in Virginia City's African American neighborhood. In a short time, other black women on C Street began three new hairdressing parlors. The next year, Sarah Miner, who inherited her husband's furniture hauling company, built it into a $6,000 enterprise. When a fire destroyed it, she was able to rebuild it the next year.

In Virginia City, African American businessman William Brown opened the Boston Saloon in

Nellie Brown
OR
The Jealous Wife

WITH OTHER SKETCHES

Thomas Detter

INTRODUCTION BY
Frances Smith Foster

THOMAS DETTER: AFRICAN AMERICAN NOVELIST

Thomas Detter (1826–?) was a wealthy and talented African American. But his life had some sharp ups and downs. Born in Maryland, he became a minister of the AME church. He then rushed off to dig gold in California and became successful in real estate and business. In 1871, he published a novel that featured some daringly independent women, titled *Nellie Brown, or the Jealous Wife and Other Sketches*. It was one of the first novels written by an African American to be published in the United States. Detter spent much of his life living in the frontier settlement of Elko, Nevada, and working full-time as a journalist and a short-story author.

? Want to know more? Visit www.factsfornow .scholastic.com and enter the keyword **Nevada**.

MINI-BIO

WILLIAM A. G. BROWN: AFRICAN AMERICAN ENTREPRENEUR

Born and educated in Massachusetts, William A. G. Brown (c. 1833–1893) moved to Virginia City in 1862. He worked as a shoe polisher until 1864, when he was able to start his own business. He named it the Boston Saloon, after Massachusetts's capital city. Catering to African Americans, the Boston Saloon flourished in the heart of the city's entertainment district until 1875. Brown went on to operate other saloons for blacks in the area.

Want to know more? Visit www.factsfornow.scholastic.com and enter the keyword **Nevada**.

1864. As an upscale place to eat, drink, and socialize, it was an important center for the black community. Archaeologists began digging at the saloon site in 1997. Among the items they found are ornate crystal glassware, beads from fancy dresses, bones from expensive cuts of meat, and the oldest known bottle of Tabasco. It seems that the Boston Saloon was one of the finer establishments in town—a place where well-to-do patrons could enjoy an elegant evening.

THE PONY EXPRESS

By 1860, about half a million people lived west of the Rocky Mountains. These people needed a reliable mail service, and the Pony Express was begun to help fill that need. Its young riders tore across deserts, mountains,

A Pony Express rider on his route

and plains at full gallop with their bags of mail.

Their route was a 1,966-mile (3,164-km) stretch between Sacramento, California, and St. Joseph, Missouri. Along the way were stations where the rider mounted a fresh horse before quickly dashing off again.

As famous as it was, the Pony Express lasted for only 18 months—from April 1860 to October 1861. It closed down when a **transcontinental** telegraph line opened. Telegraphs provided a high-speed way to send messages, so the volume of mail dramatically declined.

About 30 Pony Express station sites have been pinpointed in Nevada. Today's Highway 50 roughly follows the riders' route across the state. Travelers can follow the Pony Express National Historic Trail through Nevada and seven other states.

INDIAN LANDS

The silver boom wreaked havoc on Nevada's Native Americans. Virginia City, for example, was in Washoe territory. White settlers cut down piñon pine trees for **mineshaft** supports, fuel, and boomtown buildings. River valleys, rich with wildlife and edible plants, were cleared to make farms. Most Washoe ended up working for white people in cities and on farms.

In the Pyramid Lake area, settlers felled pine trees, drew on local water supplies, and cleared Paiute hunting grounds. Both whites and Indians killed each other. This led to the Paiute War, or Pyramid Lake War, of 1860. Neither side was the clear winner. To help keep the peace, the U.S. Army built Fort Churchill near Silver Springs.

In 1889, a Northern Paiute **shaman** named Wovoka (also known as Jack Wilson) had a vision in which he saw dead Indians rising up and taking back their lands. To make this vision come true, Indians were to revive

Pony Express riders were required to weigh less than 125 pounds (57 kilograms)! In 1850, the average man in the United States weighed about 145 pounds (66 kg). Today, the average is more like 190 pounds (86 kg).

WORDS TO KNOW

transcontinental *going all the way across a continent*

mineshaft *a tunnel dug underground or into a mountain where miners can work*

shaman *a spiritual leader*

Sioux Indians performing the Ghost Dance. This ritual frightened some of the white settlers.

an earlier ritual dance called the Ghost Dance. Wovoka's Ghost Dance religious movement spread quickly among Native Americans, especially the Sioux tribes. White settlers living nearby began to grow wary of the Native Americans practicing this dance. Settlers began to believe that the natives were planning an uprising. Tensions grew for months, resulting in the massacre of 200 Sioux tribe members at the Battle of Wounded Knee. After this, the Native Americans eventually gave up the dance, out of fear of causing any more trouble. This was one example of tensions between the white settlers and the Native Americans errupting, causing more harm than good for the tribes involved.

The Western Shoshone suffered from the influx of settlers, too. Ruby Valley, in northeastern Nevada, had long been a winter home for the Shoshone. But the California Trail, the Pony Express, telegraph lines, and a stagecoach line ran through the valley. This disrupted the Shoshones' way of life. In 1863, the Shoshone signed the Treaty of Ruby Valley—a "treaty of peace and friendship." It granted non-Indians the right to use Shoshone lands for farming, mining, and travel. However, the treaty didn't spell out any Indian rights. The Shoshone are still carrying out legal battles over this treaty today.

THE TRANSCONTINENTAL RAILROAD

Around the time when people were heading to the northwest Oregon territory in search of gold, a proposal was made to establish a railroad that connected the eastern states of the United States to the western territories. The hope was to establish the railroad in order to help U.S. expansion to the west. It would also shorten the travel time to newly established silver mines. What followed were the beginnings of one of America's most promising undertakings: the Transcontinental Railroad.

Construction of the railroad began in 1862, using money from the U.S. government. The railroad would consist of several routes and railways, spanning coast to coast across the Great Plains, the Rockies and valleys, and, thus, connecting once distant places such as New York and California to one another. The Great Northern Railway would connect Minnesota to the Pacific Northwest. The Northern Pacific Railway would also help connect Lake Superior to the Pacific. The Union Pacific Railway would connect Omaha to the central Pacific, near Sacramento, California. The Rock Island line would connect Memphis, Tennessee, to New Mexico, and the Santa Fe Railway would connect Topeka, Kansas, to Los Angeles. The Transcontinental Railroad was not just an essential addition to the country, but also to Nevada, especially during the silver boom. Many of these lines passed through Nevada, which brought new settlers and prospectors to help cultivate the land in Nevada. For many years after its first rail runs, the Transcontinental Railroad helped transport new settlers to the western territories, including Nevada.

FORTUNES FALLING AND RISING AGAIN

The silver boom couldn't last forever. In 1873, Congress passed the Coinage Act, which eliminated the silver dollar in U.S. currency. The price of silver took a dive, and the Comstock mines began to close down. In addition, tons of ore were lost through inefficient mining methods. By about 1880, the Comstock Lode was considered more or less mined out. Thousands of people lost their jobs and left the state. Many of the old boomtowns became ghost towns, with abandoned buildings left to fall into ruin.

Nevada's fortunes turned around in 1900 with a second mining boom. That's when rich silver deposits were discovered in Tonopah. In 1902, prospectors found gold in Goldfield. Copper was discovered in Ruth and Kimberly, too. Suddenly, Nevada was back in the mining business, and a flood of miners poured in again.

Nevada's agriculture also got a boost in the early 1900s. The Newlands Irrigation Project, completed in 1907, constructed dams on the Carson and Truckee rivers. The dams created **reservoirs**, and canals brought water from the reservoirs to farms. In the Fallon area, dry desert land blossomed into productive farmland. This was the nation's first federal irrigation project.

Ranching expanded in the early 1900s, too. New railroad lines were built to reach the mining areas. These same railroads made it easy for ranchers to ship out their beef to other states and territories in the United States. And new farmland meant farmers could

Q8 WHAT BECAME OF THE WEALTH FROM THE COMSTOCK LODE?

A8 Some of the wealth helped build up Nevada, but much of it ended up in California. Many businesspeople used their profits to build hotels, banks, and mansions in San Francisco. Others used their wealth to finance the Central Pacific Railroad. For George Hearst, the Comstock Lode helped him build the largest mining company in the country. His son, William Randolph Hearst, founded the Hearst publishing empire.

WORD TO KNOW

reservoirs *artificial lakes created for water storage*

grow more hay as winter food for the cattle.

Since the 1860s, gambling had been legal in Nevada. Miners burst into saloons and headed for the card tables, their pockets full of silver nuggets and gold dust. In 1910, some citizens managed to get gambling banned in the state. Nevertheless, Nevada's gambling tradition was hard to break, and illegal gambling continued. In time, the gambling industry would play a major role in Nevada's growth.

The bustling town of Goldfield was founded after gold was discovered in nearby hills.

FERMINIA SARRAS: THE COPPER QUEEN

"A Spanish lady of royal blood"— that's how Ferminia Sarras (1840–1915) described herself. Her description was not far from the truth. Sarras was born into a noble family in Nicaragua, in Central America. Around 1881, she struck out for Nevada, determined to get rich as a miner. Wearing pants and boots when she went out prospecting, Sarras made one copper discovery after another. Her many copper mines earned her a fabulous fortune. The town of Mina was named in her honor.

❓ **Want to know more?** Visit www.factsfornow.scholastic.com and enter the keyword **Nevada**.

READ ABOUT

This is the town of Rawhide as it appeared in the early 1900s. It was one of many communities that thrived as more people moved west.

1905

Las Vegas is founded

1914

Women in Nevada gain the right to vote

▲**1931**

Gambling is made legal in Nevada

CHAPTER FIVE

MORE MODERN TIMES

★

IN THE 1930S, THOUSANDS OF PEOPLE ONCE AGAIN SWARMED INTO NEVADA. This time, they were fortune hunters of a different kind. They hoped to get jobs building the Hoover Dam on the Colorado River. The nation's Great Depression was going on, and people across the country were unemployed. Men lined up for blocks to apply for jobs on one of the largest construction projects in history.

1936 ▲

Boulder Dam (now Hoover Dam) is completed

1951 ▶

The testing of nuclear weapons begins in southern Nevada

2013

The U.S. government approves a new pipeline for bringing water into Las Vegas

MINI-BIO

YONEMA "BILL" TOMIYASU: FRESH FOODS IN THE DESERT

Tomatoes, watermelons, carrots—these were some of the fresh foods that Hoover Dam workers ate. The foods came from local farmer Yonema "Bill" Tomiyasu (1882–1969). Born in Japan, Tomiyasu arrived in southern Nevada in 1914. At the time, much of the state's fresh produce was shipped in from other areas. So Tomiyasu began experimenting with food crops. Eventually, he developed farming techniques that made fruits and vegetables grow in the desert. Many plants that Tomiyasu originally developed are still thriving today.

 Want to know more? Visit www.factsfornow .scholastic.com and enter the keyword **Nevada**.

BUILDING AND SURVIVING

Construction on the dam began in 1931. At first, many workers lived in tents or shacks near the construction site. One worker said his shack town "had a population of maybe, oh, a thousand people. And the shacks were built out of most anything—tin cans, cardboard boxes, piano boxes, anything that they could find to live in." Finally, Boulder City was built to house many of the workers. In all, it took 21,000 workers to build the dam. Many workers and their families settled in Nevada after the dam was completed in 1936.

The Great Depression was an age of great strife and extremely tough times. Aside from the average person's struggle, certain industries themselves had trouble dealing

These homes in Boulder City were built by the U.S. government as housing for people who worked on the Hoover Dam.

with an unstable, and often unpredictable, market. The Depression was hard on Nevada's mining and agriculture industries, which, even during good economic times, were boom-or-bust industries. To boost the economy, Nevada made gambling legal again in 1931. The center of the gambling industry was in Reno. Soon **casinos** slowly began to spring up in the dry little railroad town of Las Vegas, but it would be years before Las Vegas overtook Reno as the "gambling capital of the world." Aside from gambling, Nevada received a boost in its economy when in 1931, state laws made it easier to obtain a divorce. Reno had been a popular destination for divorces since 1909 and became known as the "divorce capital of the world."

WARTIME AND POSTWAR EXPANSION

During World War II (1939–1945), the U.S. government opened several military bases in Nevada. These included the Fallon Naval Air Station and the Indian Springs Air Force Auxiliary Field (now known as the Creech Air Force Base). The war put added demands on Nevada's mining industry. Metals were needed to make war supplies, so people were recruited to work in the Basic Magnesium plant in the town that would come to be called Henderson. Since segregation was practiced, black workers and their families lived in an

MINI-BIO 63

FRANK CROWE: WILD TO BUILD!

"I was wild to build this dam . . . the biggest dam ever built by anyone anywhere." So said civil engineer Frank Crowe (1882–1946). And he got to do it! He became the chief engineer in charge of building Hoover Dam. Crowe invented a way to deliver concrete to construction sites by overhead cables. Before that, mules hauled carts laden with concrete to the sites. Thanks to Crowe's dam, southern Nevada grew into a booming center of population and industry.

? **Want to know more?** Visit www.factsfornow.scholastic.com and enter the keyword **Nevada**.

There's enough concrete in Hoover Dam to pave a two-lane highway from San Francisco, California, to New York City!

WORD TO KNOW

casinos *buildings used for gambling*

area called Carver Park. Nevada's ranchers also supplied beef and wool for the troops.

After the war, the postwar economic boom allowed for even more casinos to open. The casinos became round-the-clock operations, offering not only gambling, but also lavish entertainment. Strict laws were passed to eliminate cheating and force organized crime out of the gambling industry.

Nevada also became an important center for nuclear research. In 1950, the U.S. Atomic Energy Commission opened the Nevada Test Site in the desert northwest of Las Vegas. Giant mushroom clouds appeared on the horizon as hundreds of **nuclear weapons** were tested there. The tests even became a tourist attraction. Tourists gathered at Las Vegas hotels to watch the tests from their windows. Testing was carried on underground from 1962 to 1992, when the tests

WORD TO KNOW

nuclear weapons *weapons that are created from the nucleus, the central part, of an atom; when the nucleus is split, tremendous energy is released*

The Nevada desert northwest of Las Vegas was a site for nuclear testing during the 1950s.

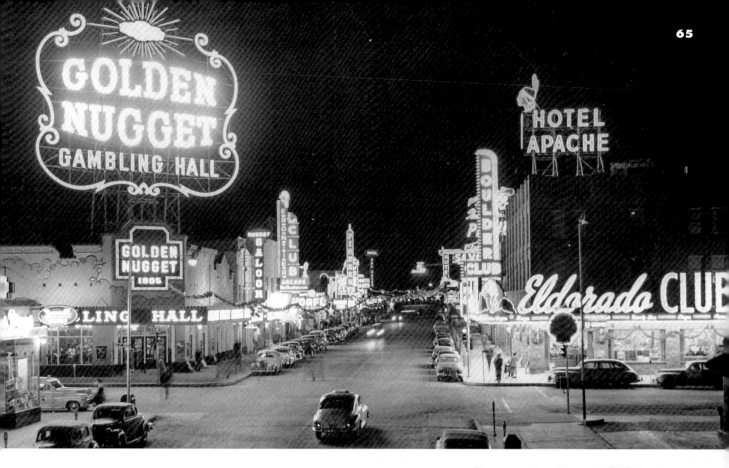

Downtown Las Vegas in 1948. Casinos offered gambling as well as live entertainment, such as music, comedy, and dance.

stopped altogether. Scientists later found that materials emitted during the tests caused residents throughout Nevada, Arizona, and Utah to develop cancer and other serious illnesses.

GAMBLING AND GROWTH

By the 1950s, tourism had become Nevada's largest industry. Tourists packed into the casinos to gamble, eat, drink, and enjoy the entertainment. Every night, they could take in shows by popular singers, dancers, musicians, and comedians.

Many popular African American entertainers performed in the casinos. However, they weren't allowed to gamble there or stay in the casino hotels. Finally, under pressure from civil rights groups, the major Las Vegas casinos agreed to admit black guests in 1960.

Las Vegas's population almost tripled in the 1940s. It grew from 8,422 people to 24,624 people!

THE MOULIN ROUGE AGREEMENT

Black entertainers such as Lena Horne, Nat King Cole, Dinah Washington, and Sammy Davis Jr. put on popular shows in the Las Vegas casinos. But then they had to leave when their shows were over for the night. Racial segregation was a common aspect of life in Las Vegas's glamorous entertainment district. Even famous entertainers had to stay in boardinghouses in Westside, on the west side of town. As Sammy Davis Jr. recalled: "In Vegas for 20 minutes, our skin had no color. Then the second we stepped off the stage, we were colored again . . . the other acts could gamble or sit in the lounge and have a drink, but we had to leave through the kitchen with the garbage."

That began to change in 1955, when the Moulin Rouge opened its doors. This black-owned casino and hotel served all patrons, regardless of color. While the Moulin Rouge was only open for a few months, it made a huge civil rights statement that got everyone in Vegas thinking. Five years later, in 1960, Nevada governor Grant Sawyer, along with Las Vegas casino owners, agreed to admit black customers. The agreement to do so was established in the old, closed down Moulin Rouge building. This was known as the Moulin Rouge Agreement.

As the decades passed, visitors continued to flock to Nevada. However, tourism in Las Vegas decreased dramatically during the international economic downturn of 2007–2009. By 2012, as the national economy improved, visitors began returning to the city in record numbers. Those visitors, however, are spending less than in the past. Las Vegans are hoping concerts, luxury shopping, and new nightclubs will bring in more money.

MINI-BIO

SAMMY DAVIS JR.: A CLASS ACT

Sammy Davis Jr. (1925–1990) lit up the casino stages in Las Vegas and Lake Tahoe with his singing, dancing, and comedy acts. He was part of the Rat Pack—an informal entertainment group that also included Frank Sinatra, Dean Martin, Joey Bishop, and Peter Lawford—and they became one of the most popular casino acts of all time. Davis was active in the civil rights movement of the 1950s and 1960s. He refused to work anywhere that did not admit blacks, and the other members of the Rat Pack stood by him. This helped bring about racial integration of high-class nightclubs.

? Want to know more? Visit www.factsfornow .scholastic.com and enter the keyword **Nevada**.

WATER WOES

Water has always been a hot issue in Nevada and other western states. Seven states, including Nevada, were drawing their water from the Colorado River. Back in 1922, those states had agreed on a water-sharing arrangement. But in time, because of rapid population growth, Arizona wanted a bigger share. The conflict finally went to the U.S. Supreme Court. In 1963, the Court spelled out exactly how much Colorado River water each state could use. Nevada was allotted 300,000 acre-feet per year. (An acre-foot is the amount of water that would cover 1 acre of land with 1 foot of water.) The issue with Nevada's water supply is that the Colorado River only supplies water to the southern portion of the state. The northern and western regions of the state must rely on irrigation projects, which can sometimes make the water supply tougher to maintain.

FAQ

Q: **WHICH STATES DRAW WATER FROM THE COLORADO RIVER?**

A: There are seven: Colorado, New Mexico, Utah, Wyoming, Nevada, Arizona, and California.

A pumping station along the Colorado River. Nevada is one of seven states that relies on this river for water.

WORD TO KNOW

aqueducts *canals or tunnels that transport massive quantities of water*

These protestors gathered in 2002 to oppose the use of Yucca Mountain as a nuclear waste site. Among them were Western Shoshone, who said that the mountain is sacred to their religion.

Nevada got busy to make sure it took advantage of all its water. It began the Southern Nevada Water Project (now called the Robert B. Griffith Water Project). This massive project was completed in 1971. It built **aqueducts**, tunnels, and pumping plants to bring water from Lake Mead to cities throughout southern Nevada. Even with these measures, however, Las Vegas still gets about 90 percent of its water from the Colorado River.

In 1989, a plan was unveiled to pump groundwater from eastern counties in Nevada to Las Vegas. For years, ranchers, environmentalists, and Native Americans opposed the pipeline, claiming the economic and environmental costs will be very high. Supporters of the plan say the city's rising population and water use make it necessary to find sources of water other than the Colorado. In January 2013, the U.S. Bureau of Land Management approved the pipeline.

INTO THE FUTURE

Nevada faces transportation challenges as it looks to the future. Current roads must be maintained and repaired, and new roads must be built. About one-quarter of state-run roads, highways, and bridges need major repairs. By the year 2025, the cost of those repairs is expected to be about $3.4 billion.

Air and water pollution are concerns in many parts of the state. In 1987, the U.S. government announced plans to dump nuclear waste at Yucca Mountain. Many Nevadans and environmentalists around the country opposed the plan. In 2010, the government killed the plan by stopping its funding. Some lawmakers, however, are still looking for ways to make the storage facility a reality.

THINK ABOUT IT!

Nuclear Waste at Yucca Mountain

PRO

The U.S. Department of Energy needs a permanent site for storing radioactive waste. The department believes that Yucca Mountain is a safe storage site, based on its scientific studies. In March 2006, the U.S. Senate Committee on Environment and Public Works reported, "Extensive studies consistently show Yucca Mountain to be a sound site for nuclear waste disposal."

CON

Nevadans don't believe enough studies were conducted on the Yucca Mountain project. They also believe it is unsafe even to transport the waste cross-country to Yucca Mountain. As Nevada governor Kenny Guinn said in August 2006, "[The Yucca Mountain project has] unacceptable impacts and risks. . . . [There are] tremendous hazards associated with transporting thousands of shipments of deadly radioactive waste across the country to an unsafe site in Nevada."

SOURCE: Senate Yucca Mountain Report; Nevada Appeal, August 20, 2006

READ ABOUT

A crowd enjoys
a light show
on a roof along
Fremont Street
in downtown Las
Vegas.

CHAPTER SIX

PEOLE

★

AS ONE PHOTOGRAPHER RE-MARKED, "YOU LOOK AT A ROAD MAP OF NEVADA, AND IT ALMOST LOOKS LIKE THEY FORGOT TO FILL IN THE BLANKS." Outside of the major cities, Nevada is very lightly populated. About 94 percent of Nevadans are clustered in the state's few big cities and towns. In 1900, Nevada had the smallest population of all the states. From 1990 to 2000, the population grew 66 percent. Today, Nevada is home to almost 2,700,000 people!

A huge neon arch shouts out Reno's nickname of the Biggest Little City in the World.

Only about 8 percent of Nevadans live in rural areas, outside of cities and towns. Only New Jersey and California have a smaller percentage of rural residents!

WORDS TO KNOW

metropolitan *relating to a large city or its surrounding area*

migratory *relating to an ability for people to move from one place to another freely*

IN THE CITY AND THE COUNTRY

Nevada has three major **metropolitan** areas. The Las Vegas metropolitan area is the largest. About seven out of ten Nevadans live there. The city of Las Vegas itself is the state's largest city. The town of Paradise is not far behind. Paradise is home to most of the Las Vegas Strip, where the major casinos and hotels are. Three other big areas—Sunrise Manor, Spring Valley, and North Las Vegas—are suburbs of Las Vegas. Henderson, to the southeast, is also home to many people.

The Reno metropolitan area is the second-largest in Nevada. Cruise into Reno, and you'll pass under a big metal arch—The Biggest Little City in the World. It's true that Reno was once a little railroad town, but casino gambling and the **migratory** divorce trade

Where Nevadans Live

The colors on this map indicate population density throughout the state. The darker the color, the more people live there.

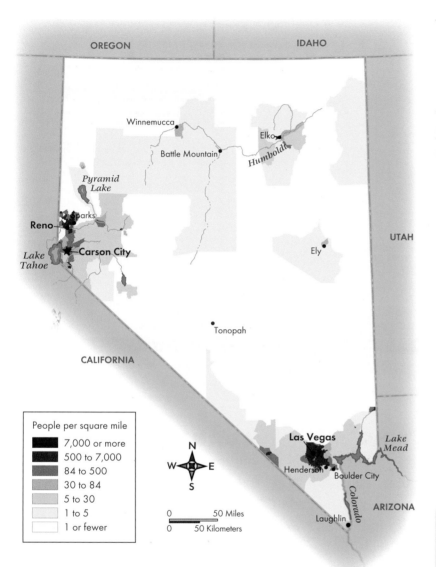

OREGON

IDAHO

Winnemucca

Elko

Battle Mountain

Humboldt

UTAH

Pyramid Lake

Sparks

Reno

Carson City

Ely

Lake Tahoe

CALIFORNIA

Tonopah

People per square mile
- 7,000 or more
- 500 to 7,000
- 84 to 500
- 30 to 84
- 5 to 30
- 1 to 5
- 1 or fewer

N
W   E
S

0   50 Miles
0   50 Kilometers

Las Vegas

Lake Mead

Henderson   Boulder City

Colorado

ARIZONA

Laughlin

Big City Life

This list shows the population of Nevada's biggest cities.

Las Vegas	553,756
Henderson	257,729
Reno	225,221
North Las Vegas	216,961
Sparks	90,264
Carson City	55,274

Source: U.S. Census Bureau, 2010 census

turned the little town into a big city. Today, Reno is home to about one out of twelve residents in the state.

More than 55,000 people live in Carson City, the state capital and the third-largest major metropolitan area. Many mining sites and cattle ranches spread out across the wide-open spaces in the rest of the state.

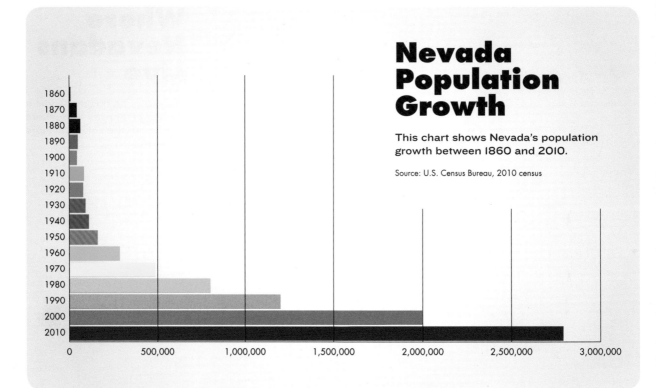

Nevada Population Growth

This chart shows Nevada's population growth between 1860 and 2010.

Source: U.S. Census Bureau, 2010 census

Q8 WHAT'S NEVADA'S LARGEST IMMIGRANT GROUP?

A8 About one-fifth of Nevadans report a Mexican heritage. In fact, Mexicans and other Hispanic people make up the largest group of Nevada's foreign-born population.

WHO'S A NEVADAN?

No other state has a higher proportion of newcomers than Nevada. More than three out of four residents were born outside the state. Some come for the warm, dry climate. Many hope to find jobs in the tourism or technology industries. And some are older people who want a pleasant place to retire. For others, Nevada offers the bright neon lights of casinos, nightclubs, and luxury hotels.

Nevadans belong to many different ethnic groups. They might be the descendants of Europeans and Africans who came to work in the mines or start farms and ranches. They might be relatives of the Basques who immigrated to herd sheep in the mountains or of Chinese workers who built the Transcontinental

Students heading to class at Rancho High School in Las Vegas. This school cost $75 million to build and has an enrollment of more than 3,000.

Railroad. They might trace their roots to Mexicans who immigrated to America from the south or to Native Americans who have been in Nevada since time immemorial. In more recent times, Nevada had the nation's fastest-growing Asian American population, increasing by 116 percent between 2000 and 2010. Many of the state's Asian Americans have come from the Philippines, China, Japan, Korea, India, and Vietnam.

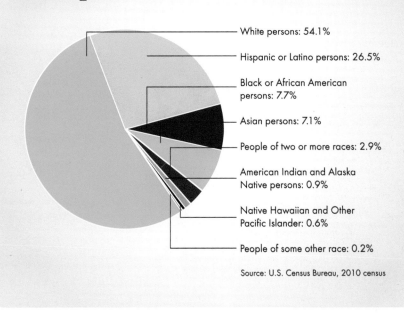

People QuickFacts

White persons: 54.1%

Hispanic or Latino persons: 26.5%

Black or African American persons: 7.7%

Asian persons: 7.1%

People of two or more races: 2.9%

American Indian and Alaska Native persons: 0.9%

Native Hawaiian and Other Pacific Islander: 0.6%

People of some other race: 0.2%

Source: U.S. Census Bureau, 2010 census

MINI-BIO

ROBERT LAXALT: SHEEPHERDER'S SON

After 47 years as a Nevada sheepherder, a man returned to his Basque homeland. His son, Robert Laxalt (1923–2001), told of this emotional homecoming in his book *Sweet Promised Land*. Laxalt grew up in the family's Basque hotel in Carson City and wrote many novels on Basque culture. *Sweet Promised Land* led to the creation of several Basque festivals in Nevada. Laxalt helped start the Basque Studies program at the University of Nevada and founded the University of Nevada Press.

? Want to know more? Visit www.factsfornow.scholastic.com and enter the keyword **Nevada**.

Basque Culture

Basque culture is a unique blend of customs, beliefs, and social traditions that may date back as early as ancient Roman times. The Basque people made their way to America during early waves of immigration, and served a vital role in the American West as miners and sheepherders. Along with the Basque people came traditional Basque foods, including *bakailaoa* (codfish) *pil-pil* or Biscayan style; *poulet basquaise* (chicken Basque style); *chipirones* (cuttlefish); and desserts such as gateau basquaise.

The Basques also brought with them traditional forms of music, art, and dance. Today, many Basques live in the western region of the United States. In Elko and Reno, Basque festivals are held every year, celebrating the cultural heritage of the Basque people.

Basque dancers perform a traditional dance.

Native Americans

Nevada is home to more than 43,000 Native Americans. Today, most Native Americans live modern daily lives. They celebrate their heritage in powwows, or gatherings, wearing ceremonial clothing and doing traditional chants and dances.

Nevada's Native American weavers have passed their art form down from generation to generation by teaching their skill to others. The Washoe and Paiute are known for their exquisite basketry. For hundreds of years, they have woven baskets, winnowing trays, and other practical items.

Lands set aside for Indian use are scattered throughout the state. Some are reservations, while others are called colonies or ranches. The Washoe Indian Colony in Dresserville, a part of Gardnerville, is home to the Native Washoe. The Pyramid Lake Indian Reservation near Reno and the Walker River Indian Reservation near Hawthorne are Northern Paiute lands. These are just a few of the dozens of Native American areas in Nevada.

Cowboy Culture

Cowboys might seem like characters from the Wild West days, but in Nevada, cowboys—and cowgirls—are everyday, real-life working people. They ride the ranges and round up cattle on Nevada's many ranches. Of course, they might ride a pickup truck into town instead of a horse. Still, their daily lives and chores are much like those of cowboys in the 1800s.

WOW

Most languages are related to others, on ancient family trees. But the Basque language is unique—it doesn't have any known cousins at all.

MINI-BIO

ALFREDA MITRE: PROSPERITY FOR THE PAIUTE

The Las Vegas Paiute group lives on only 10 acres (4 ha) of land. For years, the group was so poor that people lived without running water and electricity. That began to change in the 1990s, when Alfreda Mitre (1954–) became their chairperson. With her help, the Paiute opened tobacco shops, golf courses, and a gas station. Income from these businesses brought profound improvements to their economic welfare.

Want to know more? Visit www.factsfornow.scholastic.com and enter the keyword **Nevada**.

Cowboys and cowgirls work on ranches throughout the state.

Cowboys in Nevada call themselves buckaroos. Buckaroos get their name from *vaquero* (pronounced bah-CARE-oh), the Spanish word for "cowboy," because the first cowboys in the area were Spanish-speaking horsemen from Mexico. They came to Nevada by way of California. Every summer, they spend weeks out on the range, branding all the new calves born since the previous summer. Buckaroos get up at about 4:00 A.M. and work until lunchtime. The rest of the day is free for shoeing horses or just napping. At night, they sleep in teepees. During the rest of the year, they move the herds from one range to another for fresh grazing land.

EDUCATION

Nevada's first public schools opened in the 1860s. But few families lived in the vast stretches of Nevada's rural landscape. Most of the early rural schools were housed on ranches. The teacher would live on the ranch and teach the children of the ranch owner, as well as children from surrounding ranches.

Nevada has several two-year community colleges, four-year colleges, and universities. The University of Nevada has campuses in Reno and Las Vegas. The Las Vegas campus (UNLV) boasts a world-class department of hotel administration. The Mackay School of Earth Sciences and Engineering is based at the Reno campus. It's well known around the world for its programs in geology and other mining-related sciences. The University of Nevada also maintains the Desert Research Institute. Its scientists study weather, water, and other conditions that affect the desert environment.

ALESSANDRO DANDINI: MASTER INVENTOR

Count Alessandro Dandini (1903–1991) was a scientist and inventor. He patented more than 20 inventions, including the three-way lightbulb, the rigid retractable automobile top, and a spherical device for collecting solar energy. Born in Italy, Dandini immigrated to the United States in 1945 and taught at the University of Nevada, Reno. Dandini Research Park in Reno, home of Nevada's Desert Research Institute, is named after him.

? Want to know more? Visit www.factsfornow.scholastic.com and enter the keyword **Nevada**.

Schoolchildren and teachers at a Las Vegas school in the early 1900s

MINI-BIO

GUE GIM WAH: EAT AT WAH'S!

The little mining town of Prince was turning into a ghost town by the 1960s. But people still flocked to Prince to eat at Wah's Café. This popular Chinese restaurant belonged to Gue Gim Wah (1900–1988). An immigrant from China, she had opened the café in the 1940s to feed local miners. Even President Herbert Hoover enjoyed dining there. Gue Gim herself did all the cooking. In 1980, she was chosen to be grand marshal of the Nevada Day parade in Carson City.

? Want to know more? Visit www.factsfornow .scholastic.com and enter the keyword **Nevada**.

HOW TO TALK LIKE A NEVADAN

How do you pronounce "Nevada"? If you say nuh-VAHD-uh, with the middle syllable rhyming with "sod," Nevadans will know you're an outsider. They say nuh-VAD-uh, with the middle syllable rhyming with "lad." In fact, a special license plate issued in 2005 shows the state's name as "Nevăda" to help people say it right!

Nevada buckaroos have their own special terms, such as:
goose-drowner: a heavy thunderstorm
prairie strawberries: baked beans
tenderfoot: a newcomer to cowboy life

HOW TO EAT LIKE A NEVADAN

When you visit Nevada, you will find a wide variety of food to eat. There are traditional meat dishes, such as lomo, jerky, and pasties. And there is delicious bread. These foods have rich histories in Nevada. But these days, people in Nevada also eat fruits and vegetables and sandwiches. In Nevada, there is something for everyone. See the opposite page for some ideas.

Beef jerky

MENU

WHAT'S ON THE MENU IN NEVADA?

★ ★ ★

Pine Nuts

Lomo

This is a favorite dish of Nevada's Basque sheepherders. It's pork tenderloin with pimento. Basque hotels serve it family style, along with other dishes such as Basque chorizo (spicy sausage), beef tongue, lamb stew, and grilled steak.

Sourdough

Nevada's miners didn't have many food choices while they were out scouring the hills. Often they survived on sourdough bread. They bought the "starter" batch of sourdough in town. It consisted of flour, water, yeast, and a certain bacteria. Miners carried sourdough starter from campsite to campsite. By "feeding" the sourdough with flour and water, they could make more bread.

Jerky

This was a handy food for miners. Native Americans prepared these strips of dried meat to eat during the winter. They taught trappers and settlers how to make it.

Pasties

Immigrant miners from Cornwall, England, introduced one of their favorite foods to Nevada—the Cornish pasty. It's a round pastry shell folded in half with chunks of beef and vegetables inside. In short, it's a meat pie.

TRY THIS RECIPE
Pine Nut Dressing

For Nevada's Native Americans, pine nuts were an essential food that helped them survive the winter.

The pine nuts were eaten plain, stored in baskets, or ground up. Women ground the nuts between two stones to make flour. They added water to make a mush and cooked it into a thick, nutritious soup. Today, people of many cultures around the world enjoy pine nuts in sauces, desserts, and snacks.

Next time you're making a salad, try this dressing recipe. (Be sure to have an adult nearby to help.)

Ingredients:
¼ cup rice vinegar
¼ cup soy sauce
¼ cup olive oil or salad oil
1 tablespoon brown sugar
2 teaspoons ground mustard
¼ cup pine nuts

Instructions:
Mix the vinegar, soy sauce, oil, sugar, and mustard in a bowl and set aside. Put the pine nuts in a blender and grind them well. Add the liquid mixture and blend. Serve atop your favorite salad greens. Makes about 4 servings.

Pasty

ADRIAN C. LOUIS: AUTHOR AND POET

Adrian C. Louis (1946–), born in northern Nevada, is a Native American of Lovelock Paiute ancestry. In his works, Louis writes about life on the reservation and Native American culture. His best-known novel, *Skins*, was made into a full-length motion picture in 2002. He is currently a professor of English at Minnesota State University, where he has taught since 1999.

? **Want to know more?** Visit www.factsfornow.scholastic.com and enter the keyword **Nevada**.

ARTS AND CRAFTS

In addition to Native American and cowboy crafts, Nevada folk arts include Mormon quilting, Mexican mariachi music, Celtic dancing, Ukrainian Easter eggs, and Greek pastries. The Mormons have had longstanding ties to the western United States, as they have been based in Utah since the early 1800s. Naturally, they have migrated to Nevada over the years to seek out new opportunities. The Mexican population has grown by leaps and bounds over the years, owing to the immigration of people from Mexico, coming for jobs and opportunities.

LITERATURE AND MUSIC

The state of Nevada has been an inspiration to writers and musicians for generations. Mark Twain wrote about Nevada mining camps in the book *Roughing It*. Author Walter Van Tilburg Clark grew up in Reno. One of his best-known books is *The Ox-Bow Incident*. And children's book author Ann Herbert Scott was born in Pennsylvania but moved to Reno. Two of her most-loved books are *Brave as a Mountain Lion* and *Cowboy Country*.

Music is a part of many Las Vegas shows, and some performers have become legends. Among them are pianist Liberace and singer Wayne Newton. Other Nevada musicians include singer Jenny Lewis, who was born in Las Vegas and was a member of the band Rilo Kiley. The rock band the Killers was founded in Las Vegas, and group members Brandon Flowers and Ronnie Vannucci Jr. both hail from that city.

NEVADA SPORTS

While Nevadans do not have any professional sports teams, the state can boast a few very competitive college athletic programs. The University of Nevada–Reno (UNR) Wolf Pack football team won the 2005 Sheraton Hawaii Bowl, defeating the University of Central Florida in dramatic fashion, 49–48, in overtime. UNR also has a top-notch baseball program and basketball team.

The University of Nevada–Las Vegas (UNLV) also boasts a strong athletics program. In 1990, the Runnin' Rebels men's basketball team won the NCAA National Championship over Duke, 103–73. In 2007, UNLV made the NCAA National Championship once again,

The Nevada Wolf Pack playing a 2012 game against the UNLV Rebels

this time as a seventh seed. They made it to the Sweet 16, where they fell to Oregon, 85–77. But if anything is for certain about UNLV, they will be back for years to come, working hard toward championship glory!

Nevada has produced some fine professional athletes. Major League Baseball pitchers Greg Maddux (Padres) and Barry Zito (Giants) are both perennial all-stars. Maddux has won more than 300 games as a starting pitcher in the majors. He won the Cy Young Award four years in a row, between 1992 and 1995. Similarly, Zito won the Cy Young Award in 2000, with a record of 23-5, and an earned-run average of 2.75.

Jack Dempsey was one of the greatest boxers of all time. He was the world heavyweight champion from 1918 to 1926. Before his boxing career took off, he was a bartender in a Tonopah, Nevada, establishment.

The UNLV Rebels go head to head against the New Mexico Lobos in this 2013 game.

This freshman studies outside the UNLV student union on a warm spring afternoon.

Patty Sheehan is a professional golfer and a resident of Reno. She won three Ladies Professional Golf Association championships and two U.S. Open championships, among other titles. Andre Agassi, a champion tennis player, is also from Nevada, where he lives with his wife, tennis great Steffi Graf.

Nevada is a state filled with cultural diversity, down-to-earth people, and talented athletes. It is because of the great people here that the Silver State will continue to prosper and shine.

MINI-BIO

GINA CARANO: LIFE IN THE FAST LANE

Gina Carano (1982—) is a young woman on the move. A natural athlete, she played basketball, softball, and volleyball at her high school in Las Vegas. Carano began her professional career in muay Thai, a martial arts combat sport. She went on to perform in mixed martial arts (MMA), which allows athletes to strike with their hands and feet, as well as grapple like wrestlers. She rose to the rank of third-best female fighter in the world. After Carano left MMA, she began a career in acting. Her breakout performance in the action-thriller Haywire in 2011 earned her a nomination for a best actress award at the Critics' Choice Awards. In 2013, she starred in the blockbuster hit Fast and Furious 6.

? Want to know more? Visit www.factsfornow.scholastic.com and enter the keyword **Nevada**.

86

READ ABOUT

Governor Brian Sandoval addresses delegates at the 2012 Republican National Convention in Tampa, Florida.

CHAPTER SEVEN

GOVERNMENT

★

THE NEVADA CONSTITUTION WAS OUTLINED BY A CONVENTION OF REPRESENTATIVES CHOSEN BY THE PEOPLE. The convention met in Carson City on July 4, 1864. They saw it as symbolic to meet to discuss a state constitution on American Independence Day. Two months later, in September 1864, the constitution was approved by the vote of the people of the Territory of Nevada. This was the beginning of Nevada state government.

HOW THE GOVERNMENT WORKS

One month after the state constitution was approved, on October 31, 1864, President Abraham Lincoln proclaimed that the State of Nevada would be admitted into the Union. It was now an official state. The Nevada constitution would stand as the law of the land.

Nevada's constitution frames the organization of the Nevada state government and outlines all of the state's laws. Nevada's state government was modeled after the U.S. government. It's divided into three branches—the legislative, executive, and judicial branches. This provides what's called separation of powers, balance of power, or a system of checks and balances. In other words, the governing power is split three ways. That keeps any one branch from becoming too powerful. Carson City is Nevada's state capital. That's where the major state government offices are located.

Capital City

This map shows points of interest in Carson City, Nevada's capital city.

SEE IT HERE!

THE CAPITOL COMPLEX

The Capitol Complex began as a dusty, sometimes muddy field called the Plaza. Now it's a lush, landscaped park that includes the state capitol, the legislative building, the supreme court, and the state library and archives. It's a great place to learn about Nevada's history from the many statues and monuments. Stroll along the sidewalks, and you'll see dozens of native tree species. People enjoy relaxing and having lunch or a picnic there, too.

Capitol Facts

Here are some fascinating facts about Nevada's state capitol.

Height: . . . . 120 feet (36.6 m)
Length: . . . . Nearly 300 feet (91 m)
Number of stories high: 2
Shape of cupola (dome): . . . . Octagonal (eight-sided)
Construction material: . . . . .Native sandstone
Offices inside: . . . . Governor, lieutenant governor, secretary of state, treasurer, and controller
Notable statue inside: . . . . Sarah Winnemucca, life-sized bronze
Major additions: . . . . Capitol Annex, 1906; north and south wings, 1913
Location: . . . . 101 North Carson Street, Carson City
Construction dates: 1870–1871

Nevada's State Government

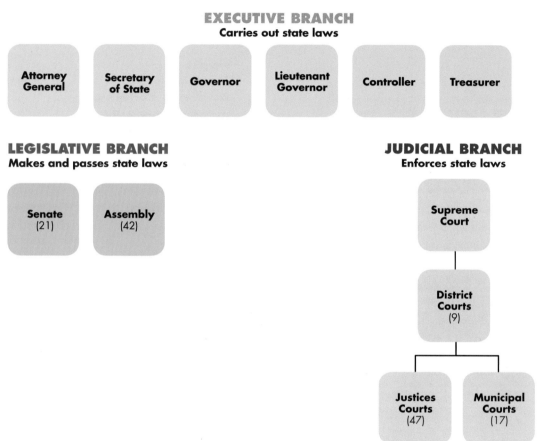

EXECUTIVE BRANCH
Carries out state laws

| Attorney General | Secretary of State | Governor | Lieutenant Governor | Controller | Treasurer |

LEGISLATIVE BRANCH
Makes and passes state laws

Senate (21) — Assembly (42)

JUDICIAL BRANCH
Enforces state laws

Supreme Court

District Courts (9)

Justices Courts (47) — Municipal Courts (17)

THE EXECUTIVE BRANCH

The executive branch includes more than 200 departments, agencies, commissions, and boards. They oversee areas such as education, taxes, and state parks. For example, the Equal Rights Commission oversees areas of discrimination of various kinds and addresses cases of discrimination throughout the state, while the Gaming Control Board regulates operations of the gambling industry. There are groups set up to review every area of the state. The governor appoints the members of these groups.

Nevada's elected executives run the government, with the governor as the head of the executive branch. Voters elect the governor, lieutenant governor, and several other executive officials. They serve four-year terms and can be reelected only once. The executive branch's offices are housed in the old state capitol.

The governor is also responsible for administering and implementing new plans and initiatives so that the state can run properly. In 2007, Nevada governor Jim Gibbons proposed an initiative to build more roads and improve an increasing transportation problem. Nevada experienced a period of rapid population growth in the 2000s. This caused congestion on Nevada's roads and highways. The governor released a new initiative to build more roads so that the people in Nevada can get around faster, and the state can continue to grow. This is just one of many responsibilities and issues that the governor, along with the other officials in the executive branch, must face on a daily basis.

THE LEGISLATIVE BRANCH

Nevada's state legislature makes up the legislative branch. Its job is to make state laws. Like the U.S. Congress, the legislature is bicameral. That is, it's made up of two houses—the state senate and the state assembly. Nevada's Senate is composed of 21 members, elected to four-year terms, and the Assembly is composed of 42 members, elected to two-year terms. The legislative sessions convene in January of odd-numbered years.

When legislators meet, they propose new laws, debate them, and vote to accept or reject those laws. If a bill, or proposed law, passes one house, it goes to the other house for a vote. If it passes both houses, it

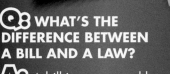

FAQ

Q8 WHAT'S THE DIFFERENCE BETWEEN A BILL AND A LAW?

A8 A bill is a proposed law that the legislature is examining and debating. After the legislators vote to approve the bill and the governor signs it, it becomes a law.

WHERE DOES NEVADA'S STATE LEGISLATURE MEET?

In most states, the legislature meets in the state capitol. Nevada's legislature used to meet in the capitol, but by 1969, it was running out of room there. The new legislative building was built just south of the capitol. It opened for business in 1971.

goes to the governor to sign into law. Nevada's legislature discusses the nature of the constitutional law in Nevada, and how laws are carried out. Members can propose new laws or amendments to the laws based on what the people they represent think, or whatever is in the best interests of the state.

Among the many pressing issues that the Nevada state legislature faces is the water conservation issue of the state. The legislature is constantly working, and re-working, the initiatives that are proposed by both the legislative and executive branches in order to establish a plan for water conservation that would adequately meet the needs of the entire state. This is not an easy issue. It is one that is going to need lots of attention for many more years. But Nevada's citizens are sure to rely on their elected officials to help solve the problems facing the state's water conservation, so that everyone will have a clean and fresh supply of water for years.

MINI-BIO

HARRY REID: MINER'S SON

Harry Reid (1939–) was born in the little mining town of Searchlight, where his father worked as a miner. The family home was a wooden shack with no hot water. Reid's childhood nickname was Pinky, and some people still call him that. Reid represented Nevada in the U.S. House of Representatives (1983–1987) and the U.S. Senate (1987–). He became the Senate majority leader in 2007.

Want to know more? Visit www.factsfornow.scholastic.com and enter the keyword **Nevada**.

Representing Nevadans

This list shows the number of elected officials who represent Nevada, both on the state and national levels.

OFFICE	NUMBER	LENGTH OF TERM
State senators	21	4 years
State representatives	42	2 years
U.S. senators	2	6 years
U.S. representatives	4	2 years
Presidential electors	6	—

THE JUDICIAL BRANCH

Nevada's judicial branch is made up of judges, who preside over courts. Their job is to apply the laws. That is, they decide whether someone has broken the law. Nevada's highest court is the state supreme court. It's made up of a chief justice and six associate justices. All seven judges are elected to a six-year term. Their major duty is to review decisions made by lower courts to see if errors have been made.

Nevada has several other levels of courts. District courts hear most cases having to do with criminal, civil, family, and juvenile matters. Justice courts deal with minor crimes, and municipal courts handle city problems such as traffic violations.

MINI-BIO

MORLEY GRISWOLD: SHORT-TERM GOVERNOR

Morley Isaac Griswold (1890–1951), born in Elko, served in the U.S. Army and fought in Europe during World War I (1914–1918). He later served as the lieutenant governor of Nevada from 1927 to 1934. When Governor Frederick Balzar died in office, Griswold became acting governor. During his short term of 10 months, he secured funding for road and highway construction and began social programs to help ease Nevadans' economic suffering during the Great Depression. He ran unsuccessfully for a term of his own in 1942.

? **Want to know more?** Visit www.factsfornow .scholastic.com and enter the keyword **Nevada**.

The Nevada legislature in session

Nevada Counties

This map shows the 17 counties in Nevada. Carson City, the state capital, is indicated with a star.

Q8 WHO CAN VOTE IN NEVADA?

A8 Today, all Nevada citizens 18 years and older can vote. But that wasn't always the case. Here are the dates when various groups gained the right to vote in Nevada:

1864—White males at least 21 years old

1870—African American men

1914—White and African American women

1924—Native Americans

1971—All 18-year-olds

KIDS TAKE ON THE LEGISLATURE!

Fourth-graders in Henderson wanted the mustang to be adopted as an official state animal. Then, the kids believed, mustangs would get more respect and protection. Nevada already had one state animal—the desert bighorn sheep. But that didn't matter. From their research, the students found that a dozen states had more than one state animal.

So the kids set to work. They collected more than 1,000 signatures in favor of the mustang measure. They phoned, wrote letters, and e-mailed their state lawmakers. Then they traveled to Carson City, the state capital. There several students testified before a committee of state lawmakers. They explained the mustang's history and importance to Nevada. Whatever questions the lawmakers asked, the kids had a ready answer.

Now the students had to wait for the legislature to vote. In the end, one house voted yes, but the other voted no. The kids were disappointed, but they knew that's how government works. And there would always be another chance to appeal for the mustang.

LOCAL GOVERNMENT

Carson City is not only a city—it's a county, too. It's one of Nevada's 17 counties. Each county elects a board of commissioners with three, five, or seven members. The sheriff, county clerk, and district attorney are some of the other county officials. Voters elect them all to four-year terms. However, none of them can serve for more than 12 years. Most of Nevada's cities elect a mayor and a city council.

For issues big and small, Nevadans know they have a voice in their government. They can elect the leaders who most represent their needs. Some people may list the environment as their biggest concern. Others may see education spending to be a top priority. And others may want to see the speed limit lowered or raised. Nevada lawmakers keep the best interests of their people in mind.

Nevada schoolkids were the driving force behind the adoption of two state symbols: the bristlecone pine as the state tree and sandstone as the state rock.

State Flag

Over the years, Nevada has had four state flags. The fourth and current state flag was approved in 1991. It is blue with a single white star in its upper-left corner. Below the star is a half wreath made of sagebrush. Above the star is a banner with the words *Battle Born*, since Nevada was admitted to the Union during the Civil War.

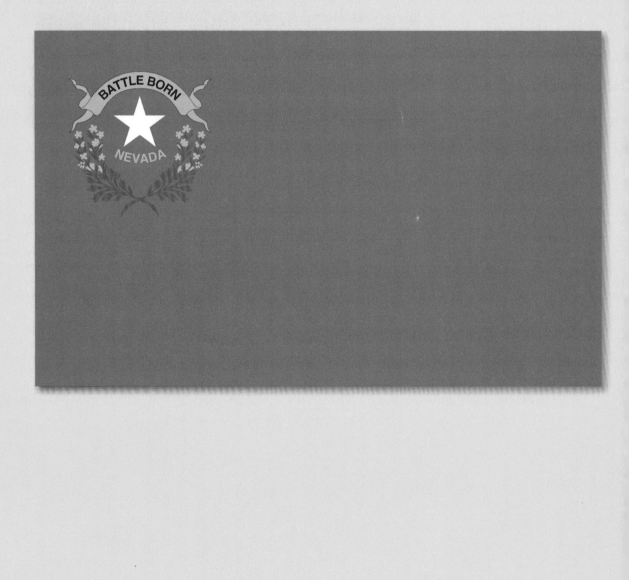

State Seal

Nevada's official seal shows a mill, a silver mine, farm equipment, and a railroad trestle, with mountains in the background. The blue seal is embossed with the words *The Great Seal of the State of Nevada* around the outer edge. The seal is ringed by 36 stars, which represent Nevada as the 36th state to enter the Union. At the bottom is a scroll with the state motto, "All for Our Country." The current seal is the third one in the state's history. The first seal was designed by Orion Clemens, the brother of author Samuel Clemens (Mark Twain).

READ ABOUT

The town of Rhyolite was founded during a gold rush in 1905 and abandoned in 1920.

CHAPTER EIGHT

ECONOMY

★

S WISHING DOWN SNOWY SKI SLOPES, DISCOVERING GHOST TOWNS, EXPLORING DESERTS AND MOUNTAINS—these are some of the reasons people visit Nevada. Tourism is the state's number-one industry. More than 50 million tourists show up every year, bringing about $58 billion into the state. In fact, because so much of the state economy's money comes from tourism, residents of Nevada do not even have to pay property taxes! Casinos, easily the biggest tourist attractions in the state, make so much money that they pay property taxes for everyone.

TOURISM AND SERVICE

All these tourists need food, shelter, and supplies. That's why Nevada's service industries employ so many people. More than one-third of all the state's employees work in hotels, restaurants, department stores, grocery stores, gas stations, and other service businesses. Some hotels are big and glamorous. Others are just roadside cabins. Some restaurants are fancy and expensive. Others are simple and down-to-earth. The people of Nevada know how to keep lots of different tourists happy.

What Do Nevadans Do?

This color-coded chart shows what industries Nevadans work in.

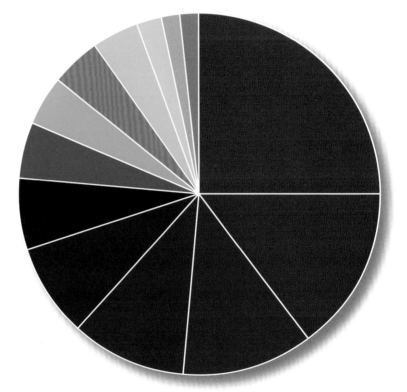

25.1% Arts, entertainment, and recreation, and accommodation and food services, 312,936

14.9% Educational services, and health care and social assistance, 185,240

11.6% Retail trade, 144,831

10.3% Professional, scientific, and management, and administrative and waste management services, 127,789

8.2% Construction, 102,463

6.3% Finance and insurance, and real estate and rental and leasing, 78,171

5.0% Transportation and warehousing, and utilities, 62,473

4.7% Public administration, 59,161

4.2% Manufacturing, 52,734

4.2% Other services, except public administration, 52,542

2.3% Wholesale trade, 28,311

1.7% Information, 20,756

1.5% Agriculture, forestry, fishing and hunting, and mining, 18,980

Source: U.S. Census Bureau, 2010 census

Raising sheep is big business in Nevada. Thousands of sheep graze on ranges throughout the state.

AGRICULTURE

Most of Nevada's farmland consists of ranches for cattle and sheep. The average size of a Nevada ranch is about 3,500 acres (1,400 ha). Almost half a million cattle roam the ranges in Nevada. Thousands of sheep graze there, too. Beef cattle and calves are Nevada's top farm products. Most of the big ranches are in the northern half of the state. Because the government owns so much of Nevada's land, many ranchers rent grazing land from the government. Horses, dairy cattle, and pigs are some other important farm animals.

Cattle can't always graze during the winter. That's why alfalfa hay is the state's leading crop. It's mostly used to feed livestock. In 2010, Nevada farmers harvested more than 1,200,000 tons of alfalfa hay. Much of the hay is grown in the northwestern part of the state. Potatoes are another valuable crop. So are wheat, barley, and onions. Nevada's soil is generally very dry, so most farmers grow crops in the river valleys using irrigation.

Major Agricultural and Mining Products

This map shows where Nevada's major agricultural and mining products come from. See a cow? That means cattle are raised there.

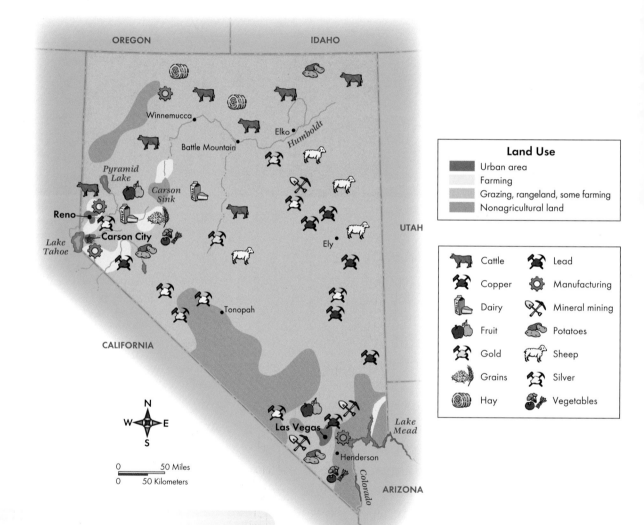

Land Use
- Urban area
- Farming
- Grazing, rangeland, some farming
- Nonagricultural land

Cattle   Lead
Copper   Manufacturing
Dairy   Mineral mining
Fruit   Potatoes
Gold   Sheep
Grains   Silver
Hay   Vegetables

Top Products

Agriculture Beef cattle, hay, milk, potatoes, onions
Manufacturing Concrete, electronics, fabricated metal products, food products, machinery
Mining Gold, silver, diatomite, barite

MINING

The silver boom helped turn Nevada Territory into a state. Mining is still a leading industry in Nevada—including silver mining. Today, Nevada is second only to Alaska in U.S. silver production. But gold is even more important to the state's economy than silver.

Miners have been digging gold out of Nevada's hills and valleys for more than 150 years. Today, gold is the state's top mining product. No other state mines more gold than Nevada. In fact, Nevada is the third-largest gold producer in the world, after South Africa and Australia.

The Comstock Lode was Nevada's mining hot spot in the 1800s. Today, the hot spot is the Carlin Trend. It's a swath of land around Carlin, just west of Elko. It's North America's richest goldfield. More than one-third of all the gold mined in the United States comes from Carlin Trend. Gold is extracted from the Carlin Trend

A miner working at the Comstock Lode site in 1868. Silver and gold mining have been important to the state's economy for decades.

mainly by open-pit mining. Some underground mining is done, too, by drilling deep down into the pits.

Gold in the Carlin Trend is not readily visible. Instead, tiny grains of gold are embedded throughout the rock. To remove the gold, mining engineers use a method called heap leaching. Ore is heaped onto a plastic sheet, and a cyanide solution is sprinkled on top. The cyanide dissolves the gold out of the rock, and the solution gathers in a collection pond.

Many other valuable minerals are hidden underground. Nevada is among the top producers of copper, gypsum, and gemstones. Nevada also mines almost all the barite in the United States. It's used to produce materials needed for drilling oil wells.

Nearly one-third of the nation's diatomite comes from Nevada. This soft, chalky stone is actually made of the fossilized skeletons of tiny sea creatures called diatoms. Diatomite is used to make filters and other absorbent material—including cat litter!

MANUFACTURING

Most of Nevada's factories are in the Las Vegas, Reno, and Carson City areas. Many process local farming or mining products. For example, meatpacking plants cut up beef and package it. Other food plants make candy, frozen desserts, and pet food. Another important aspect of Nevada's economy is warehousing, which is facilitated by Nevada free-port laws. The state does not charge inventory

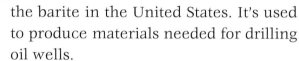

MINI-BIO

WILLIAM LEAR: JET MAN

William Lear (1902–1978) had only an eighth-grade education. But he held more than 100 patents on radio and electronic devices. In the 1920s, Lear and a partner designed the first practical car radio. This and other designs led to the formation of the Motorola company. Other inventions included automatic pilot, automatic landing systems for airplanes, and the eight-track tape player. His Learjet company became a leading supplier of corporate jets. Lear was a longtime resident of Reno.

? **Want to know more?** Visit www.factsfornow .scholastic.com and enter the keyword **Nevada**.

taxes on products that originated out of state and are warehoused here before being shipped out of the state. Nevada has several large book warehouses, including ones owned by Amazon.com and Barnes and Noble.

Some of Nevada's factories use sand and gravel mined in the state to make concrete. They may make the concrete into products such as bricks, blocks, and pipes. Other factories make local limestone into cement. These construction materials are useful because Nevada's rapid growth calls for so much building.

Some factories are printing plants that turn out newspapers, brochures, or government documents. Other factory products are electronics, plastic items, and machinery such as refrigerators and construction equipment. And where do the game machines in the casinos come from? Some Nevada factories make those, too!

GEORGE WASHINGTON GALE FERRIS: WHEEL MAKER

Who invented the Ferris wheel? George Washington Gale Ferris (1859–1896), of course! Born in Illinois, he grew up on a ranch near Minden in the Carson Valley. It's said that he was fascinated by watching water-wheels on the Carson River. The family later moved to Carson City. Ferris first sketched out his plan for a giant wheel on a dinner napkin. The Ferris wheel made its debut in 1893 in Chicago, Illinois.

? **Want to know more?** Visit www.factsfornow.scholastic.com and enter the keyword **Nevada**.

SOLAR POWER

Nevada's solar power industry got a big boost when the U.S. government gave the state more than $5 billion to develop this form of renewable energy. In 2012, Governor Brian Sandoval released a plan that targeted renewable energy as a key area for development in the state. A healthy solar power industry will bring jobs and higher tax revenues for Nevada. In 2013, there were more than 70 solar power companies at work in Nevada, employing about 2,400 people. As the industry has grown, prices to install solar systems in homes and businesses have dropped about 14 percent—a positive trend for all Nevadans.

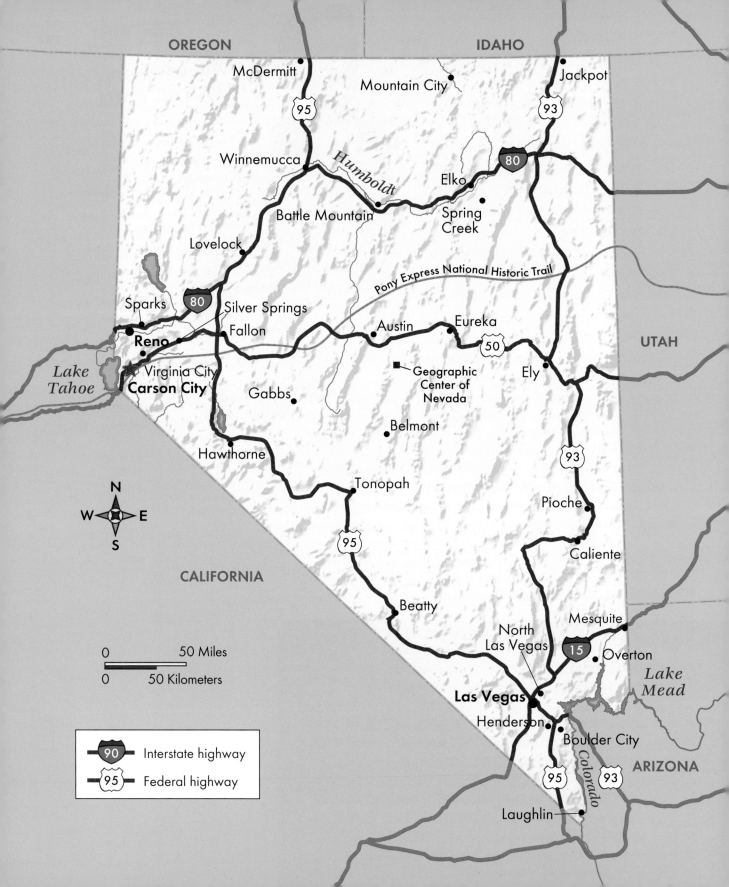

OREGON

IDAHO

McDermitt

Mountain City

Jackpot

○95

○93

Winnemucca

Humboldt

Elko

🛡80

Battle Mountain

Spring
Creek

Lovelock

Pony Express National Historic Trail

Sparks

🛡80

Silver Springs

Austin

Eureka

UTAH

Reno

Fallon

○50

Lake
Tahoe

Virginia City
Carson City

Gabbs

■ Geographic
Center of
Nevada

Ely

Belmont

○93

Hawthorne

Pioche

Tonopah

○95

Caliente

CALIFORNIA

Beatty

Mesquite

North
Las Vegas

🛡15

Overton

*Lake
Mead*

Las Vegas

0   50 Miles

Henderson

0   50 Kilometers

Boulder City

Colorado

ARIZONA

🛡90   Interstate highway

○95   Federal highway

○95

○93

Laughlin

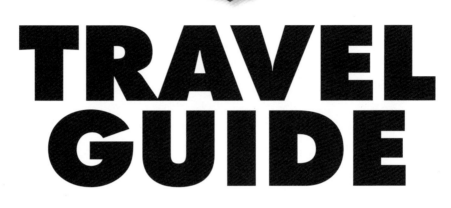

CHAPTER NINE

TRAVEL GUIDE

★

WHAT WILL YOU FIND ON A TRIP THROUGH NEVADA? Enormous stretches of desert and snowy mountain peaks. One of the world's deepest lakes and one of its driest places. You'll see wild animals and ancient trees. Visit one of the human-made wonders of the world and a city of neon lights that can be seen from outer space! But don't take our word for it—come see it for yourself.

← Follow along with this travel map. We'll begin in Elko and travel all the way down to Boulder City!

COWBOY COUNTRY

THINGS TO DO: Learn about cowboys and cowgirls and Basque history or take a horseback ride through scenic mountains.

Elko

★ **Northeastern Nevada Museum:** Want to learn more about early cowboy life in Nevada or Basque culture? This museum has exhibits on western saddles, a 1900s kitchen, Shoshone baskets, Native American Paiute beadwork, and an impressive collection of rocks and minerals.

★ **Western Folklife Center:** The center explores the American West and its many cultures. This is the home of the world-renowned Cowboy Poetry Gathering and is the site for concerts, music hours, workshops, and educational programs for children.

Western saddle

★ **Elko Railroad Park:** In the 19th century, Elko became a bustling center, thanks in part to the town's railroad system. The park honors Elko's place in U.S. railroad history through music festivals and storytelling.

★ **Ruby Mountains:** Nature lovers, this is the place for you! In a state known for its hot, dry climate, Ruby Mountains represents a surprising treat. Enjoy spectacular views of glacial lakes and impressive peaks, or go on a scenic hike or horseback ride.

Hiking in Ruby Mountains

A geyser at Black Rock Desert

Winnemucca

★ **Black Rock Desert-High Rock Canyon:** Don't miss the Desert Playa, once the site of an ancient lake and one of the flattest stretches of land in the entire world. Check out the Applegate Lassen Emigrant Trail, a significant route during the California gold rush, which looks much as it did more than a century ago.

Wells

★ **Trail of the 49ers Interpretive Center:** The center focuses on the history of the western migration of the 19th century. Exhibits explore the men and women who took a chance and headed west on the Gold Rush Trail.

Lovelock

★ **Pershing County Courthouse:** One of the state's architectural oddities, the unique, oval building is believed to be the only oval courthouse in the country.

 PONY EXPRESS TERRITORY
THINGS TO DO:
Go hiking, learn about history, and enjoy the great scenery.

Pony Express

Pony Express National Historic Trail

★ During its short-lived heyday in the mid-19th century, the Pony Express was one of the most efficient ways of transporting mail across the country. For a glimpse of what the journey was like, don't miss the Sand Springs Desert Study Area. Visitors can walk a .5-mile (.8-km) stretch of trail that passes a Pony Express station. Along the way, check out posted signs that provide facts on the history and wildlife of the area.

WOW

Highway 50 between Ely and Fernley is called the Loneliest Road in America. There are few stops along this 267-mile (430-km) stretch.

Ely

★ **Nevada Northern Railway East Ely Complex:** Learn more about the Nevada Northern Railway and its role in the mining industry by visiting the station and workshops that now function as a museum. Visitors can observe and touch several pieces of old equipment, including a wrecking crane, steam locomotives, and freight cars.

★ **White Pine Public Museum:** This museum features historic photographs, Native American artifacts, mining equipment, and displays that exemplify the rich mining history of the region.

★ **Great Basin National Park:** Set aside some time for this unforgettable park. Soak up a breathtaking landscape of desert and mountains that tower more than 11,000 feet (3,353 m) high. Be sure to visit Lehman Caves, with their beautiful limestone formations.

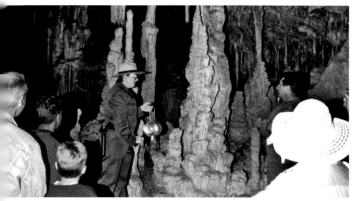

Lehman Caves at Great Basin National Park

★ **Ward Charcoal Ovens State Historic Park:** The park's highlight consists of six beehive-shaped charcoal ovens that were used to process wood into charcoal in the 19th century. Visitors can enjoy hiking, mountain biking, or bird-watching.

★ **The Ghost Train of Ely:** Enjoy an exciting ride on a historic steam locomotive! You'll pass downtown Ely, two ghost towns, a tunnel, and a beautiful canyon.

Eureka

★ **Eureka Opera House:** In the 19th century, the Eureka Opera House hosted masquerade balls, concerts, plays, and of course, operas. Now you can experience an old-fashioned sense of style and elegance as you take in the Grand Hall Auditorium and its decorative details from floor to ceiling.

★ **Eureka Sentinel Museum:** The Eureka Sentinel Museum interprets the history of Eureka. On the ground floor you will find a complete pressroom from the 1800s.

Austin

★ **Humboldt-Toiyabe National Forest:** With more than 6.3 million acres (2.5 million ha) of hiking land, and scenic views, it's the largest forest in the lower 48 states.

RENO-TAHOE TERRITORY

THINGS TO DO: Go skiing, visit historic mines, and tour the state capital.

Reno

★ **National Automobile Museum:** Explore more than 100 years of automobile history. Featuring more than 200 cars, exhibits have showcased celebrity automobiles, such as the model driven by James Dean in *Rebel Without a Cause.*

Antique automobile

★ **Nevada Historical Society:** The oldest museum in Nevada opened in 1904 and contains both permanent exhibits and special exhibits as well as the largest library of Nevada-related materials.

★ **Nevada Museum of Art:** The Nevada Museum of Art has a permanent collection that holds more than 1,900 pieces.

Looking out over Virginia City 1935

Historic view of Virginia City

Virginia City

★ **Virginia City Historic District:** Once a thriving boomtown, thanks to the discovery of gold and silver, the area is now a National Historic Landmark. You can tour the district and see the streets and buildings as they appeared in the mining days.

★ **Virginia and Truckee Railroad:** Take a ride on the historic and reconstructed Virginia and Truckee Railroad, which operates between Virginia City and the adjacent mining town of Gold Hill.

State capitol in Carson City

Carson City

★ **Nevada State Capitol:** Tour this historic old building erected in 1871. You can see the current governor's offices and explore the historical exhibits on the second floor.

SEE IT HERE!

NEVADA STATE MUSEUM

The Nevada State Museum in Carson City used to be a U.S. mint. It made coins from 1870 to 1895. The museum still has old Coin Press No. 1. On the last Friday of every month, it's cranked up to produce silver and bronze coins. And you can buy them in the museum shop.

You'll explore millions of years of Nevada's history in this museum. The Earth Science Gallery highlights the state's geological history. You'll also see America's largest exhibited mammoth, found in Nevada's Black Rock Desert. There's a walk-through silver mine, a ghost town, and more than 100 gold and silver coins. Other exhibits include Dat-So-La-Lee's Washoe baskets and the Under One Sky exhibit of Native American culture.

★ **Nevada State Railroad Museum:** Learn about locomotives and railroads at the Nevada State Railroad Museum. The museum features restored steam locomotives, as well as antique passenger carriages. Some models have been used in Hollywood Westerns. Train rides are offered several times throughout the day.

★ **Kit Carson Trail:** Take a self-guided tour of the city's historic district that winds past dozens of large Victorian homes, many of which were once owned by the state's most prominent businessmen and politicians.

Lake Tahoe

★ **Lake Tahoe:** Whether it's summer or winter, there's always something to do at Lake Tahoe. During the warmer months, visitors can hike, fish, bike, and waterski. In the winter, snowboarding is popular.

★ **Zephyr Cove:** During the summer months, sail the waters on a trimaran, a type of sailboat. In the winter, stop by Zephyr Cove Snowmobile Center for a scenic snowmobile ride.

PIONEER TERRITORY

THINGS TO DO: Tour ghost towns and historic mining towns, where gold and silver fortunes were won and lost.

Pioche

★ **Pioche Historic Mining Town:** Visit the 1872 Million Dollar Courthouse and the Lincoln County Historical Museum, which features Native American and Chinese displays, as well as mining tools.

Tonopah

★ **Tonopah Mining Park:** For a taste of what it was like to be a miner, visit Tonopah Mining Park. Visitors can walk through a mine tunnel and look down a lit mine shaft.

★ **Central Nevada Museum:** Learn more about the mining and ghost town history of central Nevada, as well as the history of the gold rush and pioneering age.

Berlin Ghost Town at Berlin-Ichthyosaur State Park

Berlin

★ **Berlin-Ichthyosaur State Park:** Visit this historic ghost town, and you'll also find an enclosed archaeological site where archaeologists are still digging for giant reptiles called ichthyosaurs.

Belmont

★ **Belmont Courthouse State Historic Park:** Tour this abandoned courthouse situated right in the middle of one of the oldest and most well-known ghost towns in Nevada.

Rhyolite

★ **Goldwell Open Air Museum:** Don't miss this bizarre collection of metal sculptures, including ghostly white figures, a steel prospector with a penguin, and a tangle of chrome car parts.

★ **Death Valley National Park:** This awesome desert landscape is mostly in California. But the Nevada entrance is just a few miles west of Rhyolite.

LAS VEGAS TERRITORY

THINGS TO DO: Marvel at magicians and have fun at theme parks. Go shopping and sightseeing.

Las Vegas

★ **Las Vegas Strip:** On this famed road, you can catch a glimpse of just about everything and anything. From a spirited pirate ship battle, an erupting volcano, and a spectacular laser light water show to themed hotels based on world locales such as Egypt and Paris. Take in a magic show, a musical, or one of many circus acts.

WHAT ARE SOME OF LAS VEGAS'S NICKNAMES?

- America's Playground
- City of Lights
- Entertainment Capital of the World
- Glitter Gulch
- The City That Never Sleeps

★ **National Atomic Testing Museum:** The Atomic Testing Museum chronicles the 50-year history of the Nevada Test Site and its importance during the cold war. Past exhibits have included *100 Suns*, a collection of photographs exploring America's nuclear tests from the 1940s to 1960s.

★ **Nevada State Museum:** Learn all about the history of Nevada and the Mojave Desert. Many exhibits focus on Native American artifacts and change often.

Madame Tussauds Las Vegas

★ **Madame Tussauds Las Vegas:** Madame Tussauds Las Vegas features lifelike re-creations of more than 100 celebrities. Take advantage of several interactive experiences, including a setup with an *American Idol* theme in which visitors can perform among wax figures of the show's judges.

★ **M&M's World:** Find M&Ms in colors you've never seen before! This four-story wonderland has more M&Ms novelties than you can imagine such as mugs, clothing, and figurines.

★ **Red Rock Canyon National Conservation Area:** Wildlife, including bighorn sheep and wild burros, abounds in this region. Visitors can participate in all sorts of outdoor activities, including hiking, biking, or rock climbing.

★ **Spring Mountain Ranch State Park:** Once owned by billionaire aviator Howard Hughes, this state park is now a shady retreat, where visitors can enjoy outdoor concerts and performances in the summertime.

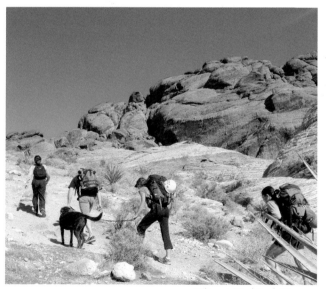

Hiking in Red Rock Canyon

★ **Discovery Children's Museum:** This museum houses more than 100 hands-on exhibits in one of the country's largest children's museums!

Henderson

★ **Ethel M Chocolate Factory:** Watch the candy-making process, from caramel fillings to foil wrapping. Then munch on free samples as you stroll through the cactus garden in back!

Overton

★ **Lost City Museum:** This museum displays artifacts, such as pottery from Anasazi Indian sites. You'll learn about the area's original inhabitants and the arrival of European settlers.

Boulder City

★ **Hoover Dam:** A 726-foot (221-m) concrete structure that creates Lake Mead, this dam is considered by many as one of the human-made wonders of the world. It offers tours of its electricity-producing system, which was completed in 1935.

WRITING PROJECTS

Check out these ideas for creating campaign brochures and writing you-are-there editorials. You can also research the paths of early explorers and settlers.

118

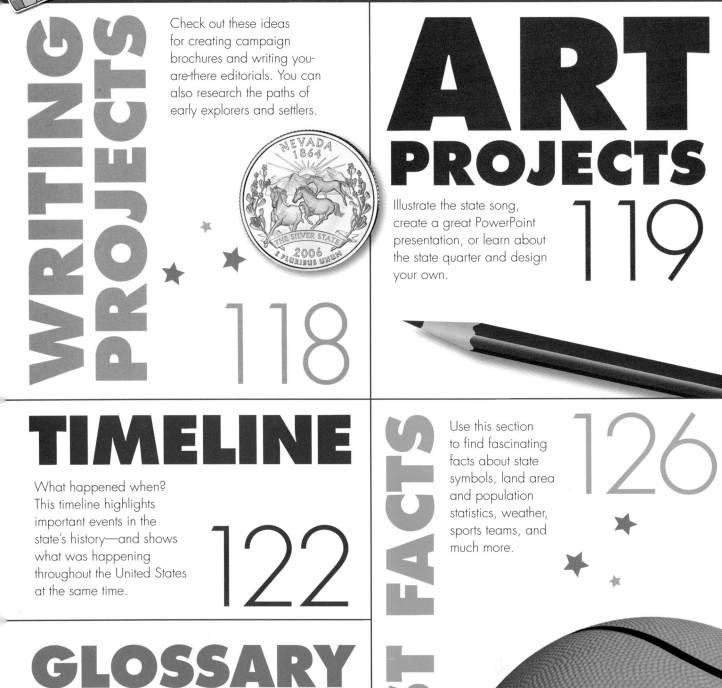

ART PROJECTS 119

Illustrate the state song, create a great PowerPoint presentation, or learn about the state quarter and design your own.

TIMELINE

What happened when? This timeline highlights important events in the state's history—and shows what was happening throughout the United States at the same time.

122

FAST FACTS

Use this section to find fascinating facts about state symbols, land area and population statistics, weather, sports teams, and much more.

126

GLOSSARY

Remember the Words to Know from the chapters in this book? They're all collected here.

125

SCIENCE, TECHNOLOGY, ENGINEERING, & MATH PROJECTS

120

Make weather maps, graph population statistics, and research endangered species that live in the state.

PRIMARY VS. SECONDARY SOURCES

121

So what are primary and secondary sources and what's the diff? This section explains all that and where you can find them.

BIOGRAPHICAL DICTIONARY

133

This at-a-glance guide highlights some of the state's most important and influential people. Visit this section and read up about their contributions to the state, the country, and the world.

RESOURCES

Books and much more. Take a look at these additional sources for information about the state.

138

WRITING PROJECTS

Write a Memoir, Journal, or Editorial for Your School Newspaper!

Picture Yourself . . .

★ . . . as a mail carrier on the Pony Express, riding across valleys and plains with bags of mail. Write a journal about your day working on the Pony Express. What types of things did you see on the trail? What types of people did you meet? Did anything extraordinary happen on your route? What kinds of adventures did you have?
   SEE: Chapter Four, pages 54–55.

★ . . . crossing Nevada in a wagon train. Write a journal explaining the hardships you might endure on the trail.
   SEE: Chapter Three, pages 41–42.

★ . . . as a miner in Virginia City during the silver boom. What was life like as a miner? What did you find in the mines? What kind of danger was there?
   SEE: Chapter Four, pages 48–51.

Create an Election Brochure or Web Site!

Run for office!

You've read throughout this book about some of the issues that concern Nevada today. As a candidate for governor of Nevada, create a campaign brochure or Web site. Explain how you meet the qualifications to be governor of Nevada. Talk about the three or four major issues you'll focus on if you are elected. Remember, you'll be responsible for Nevada's budget. How would you spend the taxpayers' money?

SEE: Chapter Seven, pages 90–91.

Compare and Contrast: When, Why, and How Did They Come?

Compare the migration and explorations of the first Native people and the first Europeans. Tell about:

1. When their migrations began
2. How they traveled
3. Why they migrated
4. Where their journeys began and ended
5. What they found when they arrived

SEE: Chapters Two and Three, pages 22–45.

Pioneers

ART PROJECTS

Create a PowerPoint Presentation or Visitors' Guide

Welcome to Nevada!

Nevada is a great place to visit and to live! From its natural beauty to its bustling cities and historic sites, there's plenty to see and do. In your PowerPoint presentation or brochure, highlight 10 to 15 of Nevada's amazing landmarks. Be sure to include:

★ a map of the state showing where these sites are located

★ photos, illustrations, Web links, natural history facts, geographic stats, climate and weather, plant and wildlife, recent discoveries

SEE: Chapter Nine, pages 106–115.

Illustrate the Lyrics to the Nevada State Song ("Home Means Nevada")

Use markers, paints, photos, collages, colored pencils, or computer graphics to illustrate the lyrics to "Home Means Nevada," the state song. Turn your illustrations into a picture book, or scan them into a PowerPoint and add music!

SEE: The lyrics to "Home Means Nevada" on page **128**.

State Quarter Project

From 1999 to 2008, the U.S. Mint introduced new quarters commemorating each of the 50 states in the order that they were admitted into the Union. Each state's quarter features a unique design on its reverse, or back.

GO TO: www.factsfornow.scholastic.com. Enter the keyword **Nevada** and look for the link to the Nevada quarter.

Research and write an essay explaining:

★ the significance of each image

★ who designed the quarter

★ who chose the final design

Design your own Nevada state quarter. What images would you choose for the reverse?

★ Make a poster showing the Nevada quarter and label each image.

SCIENCE, TECHNOLOGY, ENGINEERING, & MATH PROJECTS

Graph Population Trends!

★ Compare population statistics (such as ethnic background, birth, death, and literacy rates) in Nevada's counties or major cities.

★ In your graph or chart, look at population density, and write sentences describing what the population statistics show; graph one set of population statistics, and write a paragraph explaining what the graphs reveal.

SEE: Chapter Six, pages 72–78.

Create a Weather Map of Nevada!

Use your knowledge of Nevada's geography to research and identify conditions that result in specific weather events, including thunderstorms and sandstorms. What is it about the geography of Nevada that makes it vulnerable to things such as sandstorms? Create a weather map or poster that shows the weather patterns over the state. To accompany your map, explain the technology used to measure weather phenomenon such as sandstorms, and provide data.

SEE: Chapter One, pages 15–16.

Track Endangered Species

Using your knowledge of Nevada's wildlife, research which animals and plants are endangered or threatened.

★ Find out what the state is doing to protect these species.

★ Chart known populations of the animals and plants, and report on changes in certain geographical areas

SEE: Chapter One, pages 20–21.

Basque dancers

PRIMARY VS. SECONDARY SOURCES

What's the Diff?

Your teacher may require at least one or two primary sources and one or two secondary sources for your assignment. So, what's the difference between the two?

★ **Primary sources are original.** You are reading the actual words of someone's diary, journal, letter, autobiography, or interview. Primary sources can also be photographs, maps, prints, cartoons, news/film footage, posters, first-person newspaper articles, drawings, musical scores, and recordings. By the way, when you conduct a survey, interview someone, shoot a video, or take photographs to include in a project—you are creating primary sources!

★ **Secondary sources are what you find in encyclopedias, textbooks, articles, biographies, and almanacs.** These are written by a person or group of people who tell about something that happened to someone else. Secondary sources also recount what another person said or did. This book is an example of a secondary source.

Now that you know what primary sources are—where can you find them?

★ **Your school or local library:** Check the library catalog for collections of original writings, government documents, musical scores, and so on. Some of this material may be stored on microfilm.

★ **Historical societies:** These organizations keep historical documents, photographs, and other materials. Staff members can help you find what you are looking for. History museums are also great places to see primary sources firsthand.

★ **The Internet:** There are lots of sites that have primary sources you can download and use in a project or assignment.

TIMELINE

★ ★ ☆

U.S. Events — 1700 — Nevada Events

1776

Thirteen American colonies declare their independence from Britain, marking the beginning of the Revolutionary War.

— 1800 —

Kit Carson

1830

The Indian Removal Act forces eastern Native American groups to relocate west of the Mississippi River.

1846–48

The United States fights a war with Mexico over western territories in the Mexican War.

1776

Spanish priests are possibly the first non-Indians to enter Nevada.

1821

Nevada comes under Mexican control.

1826

Trappers Peter Skene Ogden and Jedediah Smith explore Nevada.

1829

Mexican trader Antonio Armijo makes the first round-trip journey through Nevada on the Old Spanish Trail.

1843–1845

John C. Frémont and Kit Carson explore the Great Basin and Sierra Nevada.

1844

The Stephens-Townsend-Murphy party makes the first successful trip through the Sierra Nevada.

1848

After the Mexican War, Nevada and much of the Southwest pass from Mexico to the United States.

1859

Silver is discovered near what is now Virginia City, bringing a rush of prospectors into the region.

U.S. Events

Nevada Events

1861
Congress creates the Nevada Territory, with Carson City as the territorial capital.

1863
President Abraham Lincoln frees all slaves in the Southern Confederacy with the Emancipation Proclamation.

1864
Nevada becomes the 36th U.S. state on October 31.

1868
The Transcontinental Railroad is completed.

1871
Construction is completed on the state capitol.

Capitol

1873
The price of silver begins to fall, causing many Nevada mines to close.

1886
Apache leader Geronimo surrenders to the U.S. Army, ending the last major Native American rebellion against the expansion of the United States into the West.

1900

1900
A second mining boom begins when silver is discovered at Tonopah.

1902
Newlands Reclamation Act is signed in Washington, D.C.

1905
Las Vegas is founded.

1907
The Newlands Irrigation Project is completed.

1914
Women in Nevada gain the right to vote

1917-18
The United States is engaged in World War I.

1918
The state's prohibition law goes into effect.

1919
Clara Dunham Crowell is appointed the first woman sheriff in Nevada.

U.S. Events

Nevada Events

1924
The Snyder Act grants full citizenship rights (including the right to vote) to Native Americans.

Reno

1931
Gambling is made legal in Nevada, and The Pair-O-Dice Club is the first casino to open on Highway 91, the future Las Vegas Strip.

1936
Boulder Dam (now Hoover Dam) is completed.

1941–45
The United States engages in World War II.

1951
The Atomic Energy Commission begins testing nuclear weapons in southern Nevada.

1954
The U.S. Supreme Court prohibits segregation of public schools in the *Brown v. Board of Education* ruling.

1963
The U.S. Supreme Court issues a ruling on how much water seven states, including Nevada, can take from the Colorado River every year.

1964–73
The United States engages in the Vietnam War.

1980
Nevada passes laws to protect Lake Tahoe from pollution.

1986
Great Basin National Park is established.

1991
The United States and other nations engage in the brief Persian Gulf War against Iraq.

1992
The U.S. government stops nuclear tests, including those in Nevada.

2000

2001
Terrorists hijack four U.S. aircraft and crash them into the World Trade Center in New York City, the Pentagon in Washington, D.C., and a Pennsylvania field, killing thousands.

2013
The Bureau of Land Management approves a new pipeline for bringing water into Las Vegas.

GLOSSARY

★ ★ ★

adobe bricks made of sun-dried mud mixed with straw

annexed took control of another territory or country by force

aqueducts canals or tunnels that transport massive quantities of water

archaeologists scientists who study the remains of human cultures

Basque European people of ancient origin whose homeland is the Basque region of northeastern Spain and southwestern France

boomtowns towns that spring up quickly, often because of a mineral discovery

casinos buildings used for gambling

chaff husks of grains, corn, or other seeds that have been chopped off of their hulls

decoys models of animals used to lure live animals for hunting

evaporated dried up

game animals hunted for food

irrigation a method of channeling water from rivers or lakes to farmland

metropolitan relating to a large city and its surrounding area

migratory relating to an ability for people to move from one place to another freely

mineshaft a tunnel dug underground or into a mountain where miners can work

nuclear weapons weapons that are created from the nucleus, the central part, of an atom; when the nucleus is split, tremendous energy is released

precipitation cloud-borne moisture such as rain and snow

prehistoric period before written or recorded history

reservoirs artificial lakes created for water storage

shaman a spiritual leader

staple basic, essential

transcontinental going all the way across a continent

tributaries smaller rivers that flow into a larger river

tule a flexible, thick-stemmed marsh plant

winnowing a method of separating grains from their hulls

FAST FACTS

★ ★ ★

State Symbols

Statehood date	October 31, 1864, the 36th state
Origin of state name	Spanish for "snowfall" or "snowstorm"
State capital	Carson City
State nickname	Silver State and Battle Born State
State motto	"All for Our Country"
State bird	Mountain bluebird
State flower	Sagebrush
State fish	Lahontan cutthroat trout
State animal	Desert bighorn sheep
State reptile	Desert tortoise
State fossil	Ichthyosaur
State rock	Sandstone
State gemstone	Black fire opal
State song	"Home Means Nevada" (see p. 128 for lyrics)
State grass	Indian ricegrass
State trees	Single-leaf piñon and bristlecone pine
State fair	Late August/early September at Reno

State seal

Geography

Total area; rank	110,561 square miles (286,353 sq km); 7th
Land; rank	109,826 square miles (284,449 sq km); 7th
Water; rank	735 square miles (1,904 sq km); 35th
Inland water; rank	735 square miles (1,904 sq km); 29th
Geographic center	Lander County, 26 miles (42 km) southeast of Austin
Latitude	35° N and 42° N
Longitude	114° W and 120° W
Highest point	Boundary Peak, 13,140 feet (4,005 m)
Lowest point	Colorado River in Clark County, 479 feet (146 m)
Largest city	Las Vegas
Longest river	Humboldt River, 300 miles (483 km)
Number of counties	17

Bighorn sheep

Population

Population; rank (2010 census)	2,700,551; 35th
Density (2010 census)	25 persons per square mile (10 per sq km)
Population distribution (2010 census)	94% urban, 6% rural
Race (2010 census)	White persons: 54.1%
	Black persons: 7.7%
	Asian persons: 7.1%
	American Indian and Alaska Native persons: 0.9%
	Native Hawaiian and Other Pacific Islander persons: 0.6%
	People of two or more races: 2.9%
	Hispanic or Latino persons: 26.5%
	People of some other race: 0.2%

Weather

Record high temperature	125°F (52°C) at Laughlin on June 29, 1994
Record low temperature	–50°F (–46°C) at San Jacinto on January 8, 1937
Average July temperature, Las Vegas	93°F (34°C)
Average January temperature, Las Vegas	49°F (9°C)
Average yearly precipitation, Las Vegas	4.2 inches (10.7 cm)

State flag

STATE SONG

★ ★ ★

"Home Means Nevada"

Words and music by Bertha Raffetto

It was summer 1932, and Bertha Raffetto had been asked by the Nevada Native Daughters to sing a song about Nevada at the annual picnic at Bowers Mansion. She completed "Home Means Nevada" at 4:00 A.M. on the day of the picnic and sang her composition that afternoon. The song was very well received, and Governor Roswell K. Colcord said to Mrs. Raffetto, "Honey, that's the prettiest Nevada song that I have ever heard. It should be made the state song of Nevada!"

The next year, that song became the official state song. It was adopted by the Nevada legislature on February 6, 1933.

Way out in the land of the setting sun
Where the wind blows wild and free,
There's a lovely spot, just the only one
That means home, sweet home to me.
If you follow the old Kit Carson trail
Until desert meets the hills,
Oh, you certainly will agree with me
It's the place of a thousand thrills.

Home, means Nevada.
Home, means the hills.
Home, means the sage and the pines.

Out by the Truckee's silvery rills,
Out where the sun always shines,
There is a land that I love the best,
Fairer than all I can see.
Right in the heart of the golden west,
Home, means Nevada to me.

NATURAL AREAS AND HISTORIC SITES

★ ★ ★

National Parks

Death Valley National Park comprises 3.3 million acres (1.3 million ha) of the most complex geology in the United States. Owing to its warm winter climate and its extremely hot summer climate, visitors can see unusual forms of animal and plant life, as well as interesting landforms. Death Valley also contains the lowest point in the Western Hemisphere. Most of this national park lies in California.

Great Basin National Park offers outdoors lovers a chance to see many types of plants, wildlife, and topography. Especially popular is Lehman Caves National Monument.

National Recreation Area

Lake Mead National Recreation Area contains three of North America's desert ecosystems. Lake Mead's history ranges from its Black Canyon rock, more than 1 billion years old, to Fortification Hill, which is 6 million years old and a remnant of the last ice age.

National Historic Trails

Three national historic trails journey through the state, including the *Pony Express National Historic Trail*, which traces the route used for the first cross-country mail system.

National Forests

Humboldt-Toiyabe National Forest is divided into the Humboldt and Toiyabe regions and includes 6.3 million acres (2.5 million ha). Humboldt has nine divisions, and its topographical features include alpine meadows and sagebrush lowlands, both of which make for outstanding hiking and exploring. The Toiyabe region also has different types of landscapes due to its vast stretches. Especially popular are the park's Joshua trees in the Las Vegas District and the 12,374-foot (3,772-m) Dunderberg Peak.

State Parks

The state of Nevada oversees thirteen state parks, five state historic parks, and six state recreation areas. *Lake Tahoe Nevada State Park* has fishing, boating, and a gorgeous view of Lake Tahoe and the Sierra Nevada from Cave Rock. *Valley of Fire State Park* is named for its 200-million-year-old red sandstone rock, which looks like fire in the sunlight. Cathedral Gorge State Park is a rocky remnant of Pliocene Lake, which contained a 1,000-foot-deep (305-m) lake 3 million years ago. *Berlin-Ichthyosaur State Park* holds the turn-of-the-century mining town of Berlin and fossilized ichthyosaurs—dinosaur fishlike reptiles.

SPORTS TEAMS

★ ★ ★

NCAA Teams (Division I)

University of Nevada–Las Vegas *Rebels*
University of Nevada–Reno *Wolf Pack*

CULTURAL INSTITUTIONS

Libraries

The *Nevada State Library and Archives* (Carson City) contains materials on state government, history, and many other state affairs.

The *University of Nevada–Las Vegas Libraries* have information on academics and Nevada history.

The *Nevada Historical Society Library* provides genealogical resources, as well as many books and articles on the state's history.

Museums

The *Barrick Goldstrike Mine* (Elko) gives tours of one of the largest gold mines in North America.

The *Southern Nevada Zoological–Botanical Park* offers visitors a chance to see and learn about endangered animals and plants and their habitats. A popular attraction at the park is the Desert Eco-tours, which includes a live ghost town and the Old Spanish Trail.

The *Nevada Museum of Art* (Reno) is the only accredited art museum in the state. Its permanent collection holds more than 1,900 pieces, ranging from art focusing on the Sierra Nevada and the Great Basin to contemporary artwork.

The *National Automobile Museum* (Reno) has a permanent exhibit of more than 200 cars, as well as a variety of exhibits, a theater, and a visitor center.

Fleischmann Planetarium at the University of Nevada (Reno) shows realistic motion pictures of space adventures and of hurricanes, tornadoes, and other weather conditions.

Performing Arts

Nevada Ballet Theatre (Las Vegas) has brought world-class ballet performances to Nevada for more than 40 years.

The *Reno Philharmonic Orchestra* (Reno) is the largest performing arts organization in its region. It performs infrontofmore than 70,000 spectators every year.

Universities and Colleges

In 2011, Nevada had six public and 11 private institutions of higher learning.

ANNUAL EVENTS

January–March

National Cowboy Poetry Gathering in Elko (January)

Dr. Martin Luther King Jr. Birthday Celebration in Reno and Sparks (January)

Rhyolite Resurrection Festival (March)

Snowfest at North Lake Tahoe (March)

NASCAR Sam's Town 300 in Las Vegas (March)

April–June

Laughlin River Run in Laughlin (April)

Cinco de Mayo in Sparks (May)

Helldorado Days in Las Vegas (May)

Jim Butler Days in Tonopah (May)

Reno River Festival in Reno (May)

Spring Wings Bird Festival in Fallon (May)

Carson Valley Days in Gardnerville (second weekend in June)

Motorcycle Jamboree in Elko (June)

Gridley Days in Austin (June)

Reno Rodeo (June)

Winnemucca Mule Race and Show (June)

July–September

Basque Festivals in Reno and Elko (July and August)

Hot August Nights in Reno (August)

Shakespeare Festival at Sand Harbor, Lake Tahoe (July–August)

Spirit of Wovoka Days Powwow in Yerington (August)

Great Reno Balloon Race (September)

National Championship Air Races in Reno (September)

Virginia City International Camel Races (September)

OATBRAN— One Awesome Tour Bike Ride Across Nevada (September)

October–December

Nevada Day Celebration in Carson City (October)

Pomegranate Art Festival in Overton (November)

Boulder City Electric Christmas Parade (December)

Hometowne Christmas in Sparks (December)

National Finals Rodeo in Las Vegas (December)

BIOGRAPHICAL DICTIONARY

Eva Bertrand Adams (1908–1991) was the director of the U.S. Mint from 1961 to 1969. She was born in Wonder.

James "Jim" Beckwourth See page 43.

Helen Delich Bentley (1923–), born in Ruth, became a reporter and editor for the *Baltimore* (Maryland) *Sun*. She went on to serve as a U.S. congresswoman for the state of Maryland (1975–1985). In 2006, the Port of Baltimore was renamed the Helen Delich Bentley Port of Baltimore.

Charles Bock (1969–) is a writer whose award-winning first novel, *Beautiful Children*, is about several characters in Las Vegas whose paths cross.

Clara Bow (1905–1965) was a silent film star known as the "It Girl" of 1920s Hollywood. She married cowboy star Rex Bell, who became Nevada's lieutenant governor. They lived on a ranch near Searchlight.

Clara Bow

Juanita Brooks (1898–1989), born in Bunkerville, was a historian and author, focusing on the American West and Mormon history. She studied at Brigham Young University in Utah and at Columbia University in New York City.

William A. G. Brown See page 54.

Kurt (1978–) and Kyle (1985–) Busch are brothers who are race-car drivers on the National Association for Stock Car Auto Racing (NASCAR) circuit. Both were born in Las Vegas.

Kyle (left) and Kurt Busch

Robert Coles Caples (1908–1979) was an artist who painted the people, animals, and landscapes of Nevada. His mural of Native Americans adorns the Washoe County Courthouse in Carson City.

Gina Carano See page 85.

James E. Casey (1888–1983) was the founder of United Parcel Service (UPS). He was born in Candelaria.

Hobart Cavanaugh (1887–1950) was a movie actor of the 1930s and 1940s. He was born in Virginia City.

Walter Van Tilburg Clark (1909–1971) was a novelist, poet, and short-story writer. He is best known for his novel *The Ox-Bow Incident* (1940), which was made into a movie. Clark grew up in Reno.

Samuel Langhorne Clemens (1835–1910) is a beloved author who wrote under the name Mark Twain. He took on this name while working as a reporter in Virginia City.

Henry Comstock (1820–1870) was a fur trapper and prospector. He discovered the world's largest silver deposit, which came to be known as the Comstock Lode.

Frank Crowe See page 63.

Laura Dahl (1974–) is a fashion designer from Las Vegas. In 2006, she launched her own line of clothing, now worn by many female Hollywood celebrities.

Abby Dalton (1935–) was born in Las Vegas as Maureen Wasden. She is an actor who appeared in a dozen movies, as well as the TV series *Falcon Crest*.

Alessandro Dandini See page 79.

Dat-So-La-Lee See page 28.

Sammy Davis Jr. See page 66.

Thomas Dekker (1987–) is a film and television actor and a musician. He is best known for his television roles in *Terminator: The Sarah Connor Chronicles*, *Heroes*, and *The Secret Circle*.

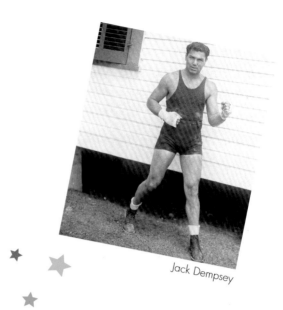

Jack Dempsey

Jack Dempsey (1895–1983) was one of the greatest boxers of all time. He was the world heavyweight champion from 1918 to 1926. Before his boxing career took off, he was a bartender and bouncer for a Tonopah bar.

Thomas Detter See page 53.

George Ferris See page 105.

Brandon Flowers (1981–) is the vocalist and keyboardist for the band the Killers. He was born in Las Vegas.

Michele Greene (1962–) is an actor best known for playing Abbie Perkins in the TV series *L.A. Law*. She was born in Las Vegas.

Morley Griswold See page 93.

Bryce Harper (1992–) is a Major League Baseball outfielder who plays for the Washington Nationals. He was selected the National League Rookie of the Year in 2012. He was born in Las Vegas.

Michele Greene

Howard Hughes (1905–1976) was an aircraft designer and one of the richest people in the world. He owned several Las Vegas casinos and other businesses, including Hughes Aircraft.

Velma Bronn Johnston See page 21.

Colin Kaepernick (1987–) is a National Football League quarterback who plays for the San Francisco 49ers. In the 2012 season, he led the 49ers to their first Super Bowl in 18 years.

Jimmy Kimmel (1967–), born in New York City and raised in Las Vegas, is a comedian and talk show personality who created and hosts *Jimmy Kimmel Live!* on the ABC network.

Jack Kramer (1921–) was a tennis champion in the 1940s. For several years, he was the world's top tennis player. He was born in Las Vegas.

Paul Laxalt (1922–) was Nevada's governor (1967–1971) and a U.S. senator from Nevada (1974–1986). He was born in Reno to Basque parents, and his father was a shepherd.

Robert Laxalt See page 76.

William Lear See page 104.

Greg LeMond (1961–) is a world-champion bicyclist. In 1986, he became the first American to win the Tour de France race. He won again in 1989 and 1990. LeMond grew up in Washoe Valley.

Wladziu Valentino Liberace (1919–1987) was a pianist and entertainer known by his stage name of Liberace. He was born in Wisconsin and is remembered for his glitzy Las Vegas shows.

Adrian C. Louis See page 82.

Greg Maddux (1966–) is a Major League Baseball player. He is considered to be one of the greatest pitchers of all time. He grew up in Las Vegas and later made his home there.

Albert Abraham Michelson (1852–1931) of Virginia City won the Nobel Prize in Physics in 1907 for his work on the properties of light, the first American to win the coveted award.

Alfreda Mitre See page 77.

DeMarco Murray (1988–) is a running back in the National Football League who plays for the Dallas Cowboys. In 2011, his rookie season, he led all NFL rookie players in rushing yards. He holds the Cowboys' single-game rushing record with 253 yards (231 m).

Emma Nevada (1859–1940) was the stage name of opera singer Emma Wixom. She grew up in Austin and went on to give concert tours throughout Europe and the United States.

Greg LeMond

Wayne Newton

Wayne Newton (1942–) is known as Mr. Las Vegas. He's been singing there for more than 40 years. And a showroom at the Stardust is even named for him. He was born in Virginia.

Thelma (Pat) Ryan Nixon (1912–1993) was the wife of President Richard Nixon. She was born in Ely.

Lute Pease (1869–1963) was a cartoonist who was born in Winnemucca. He won the Pulitzer Prize in 1949 for his cartoon "On Ripening Harvest Fields." It showed Death mowing down soldiers during World War II.

Sasha Pieterse (1996–), born in South Africa and raised in Las Vegas, is an actress and singer. She is best known for her role as Alison DeLaurentis in the TV series *Pretty Little Liars*. She has also released several country music records.

Edna Purviance (1895–1958) was a silent-movie actress who became famous when she starred opposite Charlie Chaplin in *The Kid*. She was born in Paradise Valley.

Harry Reid See page 92.

Willard Hughes Rollings (1948–2008) was a scholar of Native American history and the American Old West. Born of Cherokee ancestry, he wrote books and essays and taught history at the University of Nevada–Las Vegas.

Ferminia Sarras See page 59.

Ann Herbert Scott (1926–) is a children's book author whose writing often has western themes. Born in Pennsylvania, she lives in Reno.

Ann Herbert Scott

Brendon Urie

Patty Sheehan (1956–) is a professional golfer. She won three Ladies Professional Golf Association (LPGA) championships, two U.S. Open championships, and many other titles. Sheehan lives in Reno.

David Derek Stacton (1925–1968) was a novelist, historian, and poet who wrote more than 20 historical novels. He was born in Minden.

W. H. C. Stephenson See page 49.

John A. Thompson See page 45.

Yonema "Bill" Tomiyasu See page 62.

Truckee See page 39.

Brendon Urie (1987–) is the lead singer and guitarist of the band Panic! at the Disco. The band's single "The Ballad of Mona Lisa" was a number-one iTunes hit. He is from Summerlin.

Gue Gim Wah See page 80.

Sarah Winnemucca See page 33.

Wovoka (c. 1856–1932) was a Northern Paiute shaman, or holy man, also known as Jack Wilson. In 1889, he had a vision in which he saw dead Indians rising up and taking back their lands. To make this vision come true, Indians were to perform a ritual dance called the Ghost Dance.

Steve Wynn (1942–) is a casino developer. Born in New Haven, Connecticut, Wynn is credited for revitalizing Las Vegas in the 1990s.

Dolora Zajick (1952–) grew up in Nevada and began training as an opera singer at the University of Nevada. Now she is one of the world's leading dramatic mezzo-sopranos.

Barry Zito (1978–) is an all-star pitcher in Major League Baseball. He won the Cy Young Award in 2002. He was born in Las Vegas.

Barry Zito

RESOURCES

★ ★ ★

BOOKS

Nonfiction

Fleischman, Sid. *The Trouble Begins at 8: A Life of Mark Twain in the Wild, Wild West*. New York: Greenwillow Books, 2008.

Graham, Ian. *You Wouldn't Want to Work on the Hoover Dam!: An Explosive Job You'd Rather Not Do*. New York: Franklin Watts, 2012.

Roza, Greg. *Nevada: Past and Present*. New York: Rosen Central, 2011.

Sanford, William R., and Green, Carl R. *John C. Frémont: Courageous Pathfinder of the Wild West*. Berkeley Heights, N.J.: Enslow Publishers, 2013.

Thompson, Linda. *Building the Transcontinental Railroad*. Vero Beach, Fla.: Rourke Educational Media, 2013.

Williams, Suzanne M. *Nevada*. New York: Children's Press, 2009.

Fiction

Farley, Terri. *The Wild One* (Phantom Stallion). New York: Avon, 2002.

Johnston, Henry, and Paul Hoppe. *Travis and Freddy's Adventures in Vegas*. New York: Dutton, 2006.

Platt, Chris. *Moon Shadow*. Atlanta: Peachtree Publishers, 2006.

Reichart, George. *A Bag of Lucky Rice*. Boston: David R. Godine, 2004.

FACTS FOR NOW

Visit this Scholastic Web site for more information on Nevada:
www.factsfornow.scholastic.com
Enter the keyword **Nevada**

INDEX

★ ★ ★

AUTHOR'S TIPS AND SOURCE NOTES

★　★　★

On trips to Nevada, I've toured old mining sites, hiked in the Sierra Nevada, parasailed over Lake Tahoe, and cruised its waters. In Virginia City, I strolled along the boardwalk sidewalks and visited Mark Twain's old newspaper office. It was great to explore Carson City's Capitol Complex, too. Since deserts are my favorite natural areas, it was a pleasure to experience Nevada's landscape and climate.

For further research, I especially enjoyed reading diaries and journals of early travelers in Nevada. And nothing can beat Mark Twain's *Roughing It* for hilarious tales from the silver boom era.